A Life More Abundantly

By

Emma L. Cross

Copyright © *Emma L. Cross*, 2024

All Rights Reserved

ABOUT THE AUTHOR

I am Emma Cross, the author of this autobiography. I was born and raised in Texas. I am the author of six books and two recorded songs.

I went to Houston Baptist University. I taught at several Christian schools. I worked for two of the largest oil companies in America, Chevron U.S.A. and ExxonMobil. I was blessed to be married for 48 years to a wonderful Christian man, and together, we would do services for several Nursing Homes here in Houston, Texas, until he passed away in 2021. We had two wonderful children, and one we helped raise as our own. I am a grandmother of nine children and a great-grandmother of five. But the most important accomplishment of all was when I met Jesus Christ as my personal Savior, and He became the Lord of my life. That occurred over 50 years ago, and I have never regretted one day of it. It was the Spirit of the Lord that guided me to write all my books and songs. I could not have ever done it without His divine help.

DEDICATION

I dedicate this autobiography first to my publisher, Idris Matthews at AMZ Book Publishing Services. Second to the two great churches that I have been blessed to be members of, North Central, located at 25130 Aldine Westfield Rd. in Spring, Texas, under Pastor Emerson and his son, Pastor Larry Emerson and Bethel Church Houston, located at 2414 Lauder Rd in Houston, Texas under the first Pastor Gatlin, Pastor Cox, Pastor Wilburn, and now Pastor Rick Martinez.

Also, I would like to dedicate this book to all my family, both the Cross's the Blakeley's the Page's and to all my friends and co-workers I have worked with in the past.

To the most important one of all: I dedicate this journey of my life to Jesus Christ, the Savior and Lord of my life here on this earth.

PREFACE

This is my autobiography. This is all about my journey in this life. It consists of 27 chapters of my life. It covers my origin, birth, early years, elementary, middle school, high school, and college. It details my work history, my first loves, my marriages, my children, grandchildren and great-grandchildren, tragic events in my life and most important of all, finding my Lord and Savior, Jesus Christ, the Lord of all.

ACKNOWLEDGEMENTS

Special gratitude goes to Idris Matthews, my publisher, and to all the people with whom I have had the pleasure of meeting and working side by side over the years. Also, to all my close friends and family and the Pastors of North Central and Bethel Church Houston for guiding me in my Christian Walk with the Lord.

It is because of all of you that this book is possible.

I just want to say, "Thank you."

Table of Contents

ABOUT THE AUTHOR ii

DEDICATION iii

PREFACE iv

ACKNOWLEDGEMENTS v

A LIFE MORE ABUNDANTLY BY EMMA CROSS 1

MOVE TO HOUSTON 6

EARLY YEARS 10

ELEMENTARY YEARS 17

MIDDLE SCHOOL YEARS 27

HIGH SCHOOL YEARS 30

COLLEGE YEARS 36

DECEMBER SURPRISE 40

FINDING SALVATION 46

FIRST CHILD 48

RETURNING HOME 54

MARRIAGE AND DIVORCE 61

TRAGIC EVENT 63

SECOND MARRIAGE	68
WORKING YEARS	74
SECOND CHILD	79
THE FIRE	83
FIRST HOME	87
SECOND HOME	96
THIRD HOME	102
THE DEATH OF MY HUSBAND	107
RETURNING TO MY HOME CHURCH	112
WORD FROM THE LORD	121
ETERNAL HOME	132

A LIFE MORE ABUNDANTLY
BY EMMA L. CROSS

Hello, my birth name is Emma Lee Blakeley. I was born on July 18, 1949, in the old Jeff Davis Hospital in downtown Houston, Texas. I had four siblings: one brother, one half-brother, and two sisters. I have lived all my life in the great state of Texas. I graduated from high school and went to Houston Baptist College for two years, where I earned an associate's degree in business. I have worked as a teacher, waitress, grocery clerk, secretary, biller, and as a geological technician. I have worked for the two largest Oil companies in the world, Chevron U.S.A. and Kelley's at ExxonMobil. I then retired in 2016.

By the time you are reading my story, I would have already lost both my mother and father, both brothers and a sister, a mother and father-in-law and had two miscarriages. I was blessed, however, to have and raise two children, a boy and a girl, and to have helped raise one as my own.

One of the most difficult times in my life was when I lost my dearest friend, the love of my life, and my wonderful Christian husband of 48 years on October 10, 2021.

But through it all; I never lost my faith in God., The Lord spoke to me and said, *"Child, you are going to write a book."* At that time, I could see nothing that was worth writing about. However, as my journey began with the Lord at my side, the events in my life became a story that I believe would help others to stand firm and keep trusting God through it all.

As you read my story, you will find that the Lord gave me five other books before this one: a novel, *"Nightmare In Hell," "Welcome to My Garden,"* Parts 1, 2 and 3 and a small children's book titled Star Collections *"Spirit Power."* You can find all of these on:
Amazon.com.

Also, the Lord helped me to record two songs on a record, titled *"I am the God that Heals Thee"* and *"Take These Burdens from My Heart and Set Me Free."*

With the many ups and downs in my life, I guess you are wondering how in the world I could title this book, *"A Life*

More Abundantly " I hope after reading all of it, you will see why. For I truly believe and trust in the word of God in the book of John 10:10:

> *"The thief comes to steal, kill, and destroy. I have come that they may have life, and that they may have it more abundantly."*

More abundantly means to have a superabundance of a thing. Abundant life then refers to life in its abounding fullness of joy and strength for the Spirit, soul, and body.

So, friend or foe, as you are reading this life of mine, I pray you, too, will find this more abundant life for yourself.

First, we must admit we have all sinned and need a savior. Romans 3:23:

> *"For everyone has sinned. We all fall short of God's glorious standard. Yet God in His grace, freely makes us right in His sight. He did this through His son, Christ, Jesus."*

Roman's 10:13 states, *"For everyone who calls upon the Lord will be saved."* You must believe in your heart by faith that now He has come to live within your heart. You are now a new person in Christ. God's word says in 2nd Corinthians 5:17. *"So whoever is in Christ is a new creation: the old things have passed away; behold, new things have come."* Now, you, too, have this abundant life living inside of you. As your journey in this life progresses, you too will suffer many things, but now you have this more abundant life within you to be able to face whatever comes your way. The Lord God may even want you to write down your story so that others may receive this more abundantly life, too. Never ever forget this scripture in God's word in Deuteronomy 31:8:

> *"The Lord himself goes before you and will be with you; He will never leave you nor forsake you. Do not be afraid; do not be discouraged."*

So, you see, no matter what we face in this life, our Lord will never leave us, even in the end. Even when we close our eyes for the last time, we are assured He will be there with us. We know this because in God's word, 2nd Corinthians 5:8:

> *"We are confident I say, willing rather to be absent from the body, and to be present with the Lord."*

To keep this abundant life, you must pray, read God's word every day, faithfully attend a full gospel church, and always do your best to obey His word.

You will find that if you follow these steps, you will have an amazing and more abundant life. In God's word in Galatians 2:20:

> *"My old self has been crucified with Christ. It is no longer I who live, but Christ lives in me. So, I live in This earthly body by trusting in the Son of God, who loved me and gave himself for me."*

As you can see now, this world was never meant to be about us and our story, but it is to share our story so that others will come to have this more abundant life living on the inside of them. And that, my friend, is why I titled my story *"A Life Moore Abundantly"* Now, I hope you enjoy your reading and draw closer to our Lord and Savior, Jesus Christ.

MOVE TO HOUSTON

To tell my story, I must tell you their story, my family. There was my mother, father, brother, and a stepbrother and two sisters. At the time they all lived in a small town in West Texas called Mineral Wells which was famous for their mineral water which all the HEB stores still purchased today.

My mother's name was Emma Mays West. She was born in a town in Old Mexico which Sara Blanco is now a part of Texas. She was born on January 16, 1911. She lived with her mother, Jessie West, my grandmother

My mother worked at the time at the Baker Hotel in the laundry room. She was divorced and had one son, named Jessie Lee Hardy who was born on July 2, 1933.

My father's name was Claude Price Blakeley, and he was born on August 22, 1912. He lived with his father, my grandfather, on a small farm in Mineral Wells. He also worked at the Baker Hotel there.

One day while my mother was in the lunchroom having her lunch, my father came in and he noticed her and started talking with her. From that time on every time, she was there for lunch my dad would come and talk with her. One day he asked her out and then they became engaged and got married on August 1, 1936, at the courthouse in Weatherford Texas. After their short honeymoon, my father and mother went to live with my grandmother.

My mother gave birth to my first sister, Dora Dean Blakeley. She was born in Mineral Wells, Texas. On May 13, 1937, she gave birth to my brother, Glen Price Blakeley born also in Mineral Wells, Texas March 29,1940. On November 14, 1942, she gave birth to my second sister, Wanda Jean Blakeley, which was also born there.

My mother and father continued to live with my grandmother until around 1946. This is when my father came to my mother and said he wanted to go to Houston Texas where his brothers were and find a job. Afterwards, he would come back and get the rest of the family. So around six months later he came back for them. However, my stepbrother and brother continued to remain with my grandmother.

I was told by my sister, Wanda, that when they arrived at their destination, there were only two tents and one was for the animals, a cow, and chickens. The other was for them to live in.

My father finally got a job as a cook at the Rice Hotel in downtown Houston, Texas. Then on July 18, 1949, I came along. I was born at the old Jeff Davis Hospital in Houston.

I was named after my stepbrother, Jessie Lee Hardy because I was born in July also, and I was given my mother's first name. So, my name is Emma Lee Blakeley but in a later chapter I will explain why I wanted to be called Emily for my first name.

I was told that the doctors first thought my mother had a tumor, but it turned out that I was a change of life baby.

After me, my mother did not have any more children, so I was the baby of the family.

We all lived in the tent until our daddy rented a 2-story home close by where LBJ hospital is now. My experiences there were both good ones and not so good ones. The good ones I remembered are the following: I came home from school first and then when my sister, Wanda came home we would walk to the store and buy a coke and package of peanuts each with our lunch money that we saved. My sister still today, on my birthday sometimes buys me a coke and peanuts as a reminder of those times. Another time was when My parents gave me a cow of my very own, but she got sick and died. My mother and I buried her behind the barn. Another time is when I would hear my mother telling my dad that she was worried about me not walking. However, she did not know that I would walk upstairs to Pop who was our landlord, and I would walk for him, and he would give me candy. Later though, she did find out and she was very pleased. Another good time was I was always glad when I returned from school to play with my dog, Queenie. She was a beautiful border collie and looked just like Lassie on TV. She had some beautiful puppies, and my parents let my sister, Wanda, give them away to some friends of hers at school. I was so angry that I kicked and broke the window in my bedroom. I thought they would surely punish me, but I got mercy instead. Boy was I ever glad! Another time was when my mother and I would get down on our knees every night on the cement floors to pray that my father would stop smoking. Then one day, he came and said that if God heals his sister that he would give up smoking; but that did not happen; but he did eventually stop smoking.

EARLY YEARS

I was born on July 18, 1949, in the old Jeff Davis Hospital in Houston, Texas. I was told that every member of the family was very happy to see me. When I arrived, they said that I did not want to eat, so they gave me ice cream, and they all said I loved it. Of course, I did, and I became a bit overweight, and the doctor told my mother to limit my ice cream intake. I am sure I probably did not like that idea at all, but I seemed to thrive after all. I stayed in the tent with the rest of my family. I was told that one night, a huge storm came, but I still needed diapers and milk, so my father stood in knee-deep water to go to the store to purchase them for me.

We continued to live in the tent until I was about three years old. We then moved to a two-story duplex off Chaplain St. in Houston. I remember a lot of memorable times while living there. As I said, I was almost three years old when we moved there, and I did not crawl. I scooted across the floor. I never understood how because the floors were cement, and there was no carpet of any kind. My mother, at that time, convinced my father that she was afraid because I had not been walking yet. However, she never found out that I would crawl up the steps, and there lived an elderly man called Pop who would give me candy if I walked to him, and I always happily did. Later, though, I started walking in front of all my family, and my mother became reassured. I also remember some not-so-good times there. After we had been there for several years, my mother and father had my brother, Glen, come and live with us there. He was very mean to me and did things to me that I did not like. He would tell me if I told anyone he would beat me up. I never told anyone about what he did until he passed away. He always had such a bad temper. I remember on one occasion, he took a knife after my mother, and I had to call the neighbor for help. I survived that trauma and became stronger.

I also remember the time my aunt Gladdys, my father's sister, who at the time was living with us, was diagnosed with cancer. I did not know what that meant, but I knew and saw so much blood that day. I seen my mother put scissors under her mattress to stop the bleeding. But, one horrible day, an ambulance came to take her to the hospital. I remember running upstairs and hiding because I could not stand the loud noise, and I was so afraid. I never saw my aunt again. She passed away in the hospital. I also remember my mother and me down on our knees on the hard cement floors, praying every night for my father to quit smoking. He told my mother that if his sister was healed, he would give up smoking. His prayer was not answered in the way he wanted, but our prayers did. My father then stopped smoking and never smoked again.

I do not remember what happened to Pop upstairs, but I remember that my uncle Robert, my father's brother and his wife, Helen, moved into the upstairs apartment.

On one occasion, my mother, Aunt Helen, and I were upstairs in their apartment visiting. She gave me soda pop in a bottle to drink. To this day, I do not know why I did this thing next. I put my tongue into the bottle, and it got stuck. I started screaming and crying. And my aunt just sat me down and broke the bottle right in front of me. I was both relieved and traumatized by how she did it. And to this day, I never did that stunt again.

Another time was when I got mad and threw a hissy fit. I was on the floor, kicking and screaming. My mother did not know what to do, but I remember my aunt getting up and saying I would take care of this. She got a glass of very ice-cold water, and she proceeded to throw it all over me. I jumped up, and I never threw a fit like that again. On another occasion, she traumatized me with fire. My Aunt Helen was taking care of two children at the time, Troody and Mike. Mike and I were playing in the yard, and Mike happened to have some matches.

He lit one and was showing me, and Aunt Helen saw it, and she became furious. Now, in my mind, I do not know for sure, but I think I saw her take one match, light it up, and tell Mike to stick out his finger. She then explained to him that it would hurt a lot more the next time. That one horrible memory so traumatized me that even today, it is very hard for me to strike a match or light a fire. I will explain more about it in the chapters ahead.

Staying with more memories during my early years there, on another occasion, my mother and father gave me a baby calf after our cow gave birth to her. However, shortly after she was born, she became very sick. I remember my mother staying up all hours of the night, taking care of her and trying to feed her raw eggs for strength. Sadly, though, she did not make it, and I helped my mother bury her behind our barn. Another bad time was when my brother Glen got bitten by a rat. The story here is that for almost a week, my brother and cousin, Choice, would stay up all night with a Beebe gun and shoot rats that were found in our kitchen.

Now, mind you, the whole family was sleeping in one room there, in different beds because it was cold, and we did not have anything but one heater in the house. My brother was sleeping in the corner by himself with loads of covers. That night, a rat crawled up under all his covers and bit him on the ankle. I remembered seeing a lot of blood again. When my father saw it, he just wanted him to wash it off, put medicine on it, and let it go. My father did not believe in taking anyone to the doctor unless he thought it was an emergency. However, my mother did, and she went upstairs and asked my uncle Robert to take him, and her to the E.R. He did, and my brother had to get a shot and some stitches.

From then on, my brother used rat traps instead of trying to shoot them. Another bad memory is when I got mad and kicked out my bedroom window. The story is about a beautiful collie named Queenie. She had a litter of pups that I wanted to keep, but my mother did not, so they were given away. I got so upset that I started kicking my bedroom window. I thought they would punish me, but they didn't. I told them I was sorry, and I never did anything like that again.

Now, all my memories are not bad. I had some very good ones, too. My favorite times were when my sister, Wanda, would come home from school every afternoon, and we would walk to the corner store and buy peanuts and a coke, and we would have that every day after school. We would save a nickel from our lunch money to buy it. As you can tell, that was in the old days.

After several months or more, my aunt and uncle moved to another home not far away, and we were able to walk around to see them. On one occasion, my sister, Wanda, and I were walking to see my aunt, and she was carrying me on her shoulders. She accidentally dropped me onto some shell. To this day, I still have the scar on my hand.

On another day, while my family was visiting them, a lady named Wanita, whom we started calling sister Wanita, invited all of us to her church on Berry Road and Laura Koppy. My aunt and uncle thought it was a great idea because, at that time, they were trying to adopt a little girl named Carolyn. There will be more stories in the chapters ahead concerning her and her family.

Another strange thing was my sister, Dora Dean, was skating at the Rainbow Skating Rink off Irvington one day, and a young woman came in and invited her to come to her church and it just happened to be the same church that sister Wanita asked us to come too. The young woman's name was sister Brown, and she became my sister' Sunday school teacher and my Sunday school teacher. She was even my children's

Sunday school teacher. The church was Bethel Pentecostal Church of God, located at Berry Rd. and Laura Koppy. I was told that the pastor there, Pastor A. L. Gatlin, was building the church when he sawed off a thumb. He then buried it under the church and continued building it. He never stopped until it was completed.

They tell me when I first came to Bethel, I was just a baby. I was dedicated and joined the church at three years of age.

Our Church now has a new name, Bethel Church Houston, and on June 23, 2024, we had an 80th-year celebration of the church. We have had several pastors since the beginning when Pastor Gatlin was there: Pastor Gary Cox, Pastor Wilburn, another Pastor Gatlin and now Pastor Ricky Martinez. I was a member from the time I was three years old and all through my elementary, middle school, high school, and college years and even when I got married on June 28, 1973. Pastor A. L. Gatlin married my husband and me. I have had many wonderful and happy times at my home church. More will be said in later chapters.

As for now, this concludes all my early year memories, and now we move on to my Elementary years.

ELEMENTARY YEARS

A lot of changes occurred during my elementary years. My father resigned from the Rice Hotel in downtown Houston in 1952 and became an employee of the famous Shamrock Hotel located at that time in Southwest Houston. My brother, Glen, and my older sister, Dora Dean, both worked there as well.

The **Shamrock** was a hotel constructed between 1946 and 1949 by Glenn McCarthy southwest of downtown Houston, Texas, next to the Texas Medical Center. It was the largest hotel built in the United States during the 1940s. The grand opening of the Shamrock is still cited as one of the biggest social events ever held in Houston. Sold to Hilton Hotels in 1955 and operated for over three decades as the **Shamrock Hilton**, the facility endured financial struggles throughout its history. In 1985, Hilton Hotels donated the building to the Texas Medical Center and the structure was demolished on June 1, 1987.

I remember well those days. My father worked during the daytime, and my brother and sister worked there at night. I remember my father taking us to pick them up at night. He would have a mattress that we would lay on, and my mother, my father, and my sister would all sing songs to help pass the time away until they got off for the night. I still can recall some of those songs today. That was a great time bonding with my mom, dad, and sister.

Another big change for me was that we moved from the two-story duplex home to a huge home off Highway 59 and Cavalcade. The school that I went to was Kashmere Gardens Elementary School, just off Lockwood Street in Houston, Texas. I was in kindergarten there. I remembered how much I hated to take naps. I was so happy when I passed the first grade because then I no longer had to take naps. However, my teacher then explained to my older sister that I was very shy and did not talk much, and she thought if I was retained in the first grade, she would be able to help me to become more sociable. So, there you have it people. The only grade that I failed was the first grade.

The next year, I went into the second grade. One day after school, I remembered I was walking to catch my bus. I never looked up. I always looked down because I was still somewhat shy. I thought I was following another boy in my class who rode the same bus as I did, but when I looked up, it was not the same boy. I turned to my left just as I watched with tears in my eyes; my bus took off without me. I was devastated and very frightened, and a teacher then asked me if I had any siblings going there and that she could take me too. I told her I had a sister named Wanda Jean, and she found out that she was in the 4th-period gym at that time of the day. I remember her taking me to see her there. She was sitting Indian style on the floor like the other girls were. I immediately joined her. She asked me what happened and why I had not gotten on my bus, and I told her. She then reassured me that it would be ok and that I could go home on the bus with her. When I got home that day, I remembered how frantic my mother was, and she wanted to know the whole story of what had happened to me. I told her.

Some more things I remember while living there were: I remember I had a lot of ear infections, and I was taken to the doctor, and he lensed my ear drum. I kept having pain, and my mother would faithfully put some Epson salt in a napkin, warm it and place it gently on my ears. I remember how good it felt. Also, I remember my father would bring home leftovers of expensive meats from the Shamrock, where he was the main cook and my mother would make the most delicious meal, which she called goulash. I loved it so much. I still cook it today.

Another memory is teaching my dogs my history lessons. I would stand out on the pouch, and the two dogs would sit down and look up at me. They would stay in that position until I was through talking to them. I loved that so much that I wanted to become a teacher when I grew up. I did become a teacher. I taught at several Christian schools here in Houston, Aldine Christian and Champions Academy.

Then, before I was promoted to the third grade, my father decided to move again. This time, we moved to a home right off North Main Street in Houston, Texas.

The school I attended was Robert E. Lee Elementary, and I attended there until I was promoted to Middle School.

I remember the first day of school there. Everything seemed to be going just great. When school ended that day, and it was time for me to go home, I waited; and it felt like a very long time for my mother and father. They told me to wait there until they came because I would get lost if I tried to walk home by myself. I did not listen. I started walking and never looked up. I knew I was lost and that I should have stayed and waited for my parents to come and get me. I started to pray and then I looked up and saw the Western Auto store on the corner. I knew then I was close to home because I remembered that my father had taken me there when he bought a freezer. I wiped the tears from my eyes and found my home. When I got there, my mom and dad were furious with me and told me never to do that again. I told them I was sorry. I finally learned to walk home the short way.

After attending Robert E. Lee for a few months, I wanted badly to become one of the patrol girls. They were the ones who held poles out to allow the students to safely cross the street. I remember the teacher telling me that if I wanted that position, my grades would have to be very good. I studied hard, and my grades were excellent. Also, I became good friends with one of the patrol girls and one day, good news came. The teacher came and told me that if I still wanted to be one of their petrol girls, I could have that position. I said, "Yes, Mam, I do."

While still living there on Garden Street off North Main, my sister, Wanda Jean, was working for a lady cleaning apartments next door. While cleaning an apartment there she met a young man named Doyle Teater, a truck driver. He was out of town a lot, but when he was gone, she would go in and clean his apartment. They got to know each other very well and liked one another, and one day, my mother and father told me that Doyle and Wanda were getting married. I did not understand. My sister was only 14 at the time. However, my mother and father said it would be ok. It did turn out well. She remained his wife for many, many years until he passed away in January 1996. She gave birth to four boys, Doyle Teater Jr., James Allen Teater, David Teater, and Donald Teater. So, everything turned out well in the end.

For me, I remember when I heard the news, I went around saying, "I got me a new son-in-law," and they kept trying to tell me that it was not so, that he was my brother-in-law. I finally came to that conclusion.

After several years there, one day, my father came and told us we were moving to another home not far away, located on Boundary Street. My Uncle Robert and Aunt Helen would be living across the street from us.

I found out that I would still be going to Robert E. Lee Elementary, and that was fine with me. I had quite a few memories there. One day, walking home from school with a friend of mine, we began talking, and she asked me if I had ever been in the hospital. I told her, "No, never." She laughed and said, "Yes, you have. You were there when you were born." I replied, "Yes, that is true, but no other time." I got home that very afternoon, and I started itching all over, and there were red bumps all over me. I called my mother, who was at work, and told her how I was feeling. She called my aunt and uncle, and they all took me to the doctor's office. There, he examined me and said, "I believe she has Scarlet Fever Rash, and if we do not administer this shot, it will turn into Scarlet Fever. I did not want to get a shot. I asked to go to the bathroom, and I remembered trying to crawl out the window to get away, but the window was too high up, so I was not able to go. I went back into the office, and it took the nurse, my mother and my aunt to hold me down that day to get the shot. Afterward, I started to feel much better. When my older sister, Dora Dean, came in from work, she came over to see how I was feeling. She said she had insurance on me and that I was going to the hospital. She took me, and I had to stay in the hospital for almost a week. I remembered that no one was allowed to see me unless they wore a gown and gloves. I did not understand; I just wanted to go home. The next time I was in the hospital was when I had my two children years later.

A few months after that, I heard my mom had quit working for my other uncle and aunt, and she started taking care of four children for a single mom who lived down the street from us. One day, my father bought a pool table, and he gave me the box it came in. I made the box into a huge slide across the steps of my pouch. I was having fun sliding, and then the children that my mother was taking care of came. We all had fun taking turns sliding down the steps on the box.

Leona had four children: a set of twins named Jennie and Johnny, Gary and Sherral. The twins were around my age, so we bonded well. After a few months, something happened. I got my first kiss at nine years old. One day, Jennie, Johnny and I were running around the pool table, and after a few times, suddenly, somebody turned off the light and just then came kiss across my lips. I knew then that Johnny liked me, and so did Jennie. She would get me to get Johnny to do her chores because she knew I could. I only needed to ask, and he would do anything for me. Johnny became my first boyfriend. We became very close but never that close, if you know what I mean. One evening, his mom called my mom and asked if we would come over. She then asks my mom to go with her to pick out a tree for Christmas. She said she would be back very soon and left us all there. Gary decided he would play with some matches, and shortly after he lit one, he blew it out quickly. However, the lingering smoke was still in the room and when Leona and my mom returned, they could smell it. Leona was furious, and she grounded all of them. I felt so bad about it all. My mom and I then went back home. When I got home, I thought my mom was going to punish me, but she never did. I told her I was very sorry, but I did not know that Gary was doing that until we went into his room. She said it was all ok.

It was another year or so when I received some bad news: Leona was moving away. I did not see Jennie, Johnny, Gary or Sherral any more until several years later. I will discuss that in a future chapter.

Once again, my father came and told us we were moving back to Garden Street, across the street from where we lived before. The house was for sale now, and my father bought it. I continued going to Robert E. Lee School. I started taking piano lessons from my music teacher, Miss Bindi. I had my first and only recital at a church off Houston Avenue. I remember it well. I stopped my music lessons because she suddenly passed away. I did have some very good friends who went to school with me, and they lived on the corner from me. My best friend's name was Rita, and she was very intelligent and always got excellent grades in school. Her sister, Judy, was also my friend. All through high school, and I will add to that when I speak of my High School years. I had another very sweet older friend who lived across the street from me. She was the sister to a lady named Ramona, who was the lady who hired my sister, Wanda, years ago. My friend's name was Diana, and we became very close friends, and I will discuss it in more detail in the next few chapters.

Finally, I was promoted to Marshall Jr. High on September 10, 1961.

MIDDLE SCHOOL YEARS

Going from elementary to high school now was a very big change for me. One that would bring many different challenges to my life. I got very good grades. I was in the Honor Society and the Future Teachers Club and substituted many times for teachers who needed a break or were not able to be in class that day. On Saturdays, my best friend Rita and I would be marching in the Deputy band. We marched in many parades here in Houston, Texas. I received many awards, a future teacher certificate and perfect attendance for all three years, and I was nominated to be a typist in the school paper.

However, I never went to any school dances. I still was too shy. One day, a boy named Kenith asked me to go with him to the school dance. I told him a white lie. I told him that my mother would not let me go out with the boys yet. He tried again in High School to no avail. However, I will tell you more in the next few chapters.

I remember while I was still in middle school, one day, my sister Wanda came and told me that she was at a hospital in Little York. She ran into Leona and got her address and phone number to let me know. If you remember, I mentioned her and her children in previous chapters. Johnny was my first boyfriend, and I was very nervous about seeing them all again. My sister took me to their house, and when I knocked on the door, Jennie came out, and she recognized me immediately. She offered me the chance to come in and have some refreshments, and I believe she asked if I could spend the night with them. I did, and she told me that Johnny, her brother, had just broken up with his girlfriend. Later that evening, we all played a game called Spin the Bottle. The result was whoever the bottle landed on would be kissed by the opposite person. Guess who got kissed that night. I did, and it was Johnny who kissed me.

Later that night, he came to me and asked me if I would like to go with him, and I did not understand. Then he explained, I mean, go steady with him, and I would be his girlfriend again. I told him OK, and he kissed me goodnight and said he would see me in the morning. So, on several weekends, I would be spending time with the family there. Then, on one occasion, my mother overheard me telling Rita, my friend, that Johnny was my boyfriend. Well, that was the last time I got to go over to their house on the weekends, and I never saw him again.

Another not so-good memory was one day when my mother, grandmother, and my aunt Helen all went shopping at W. T. Grants in downtown Houston. I was with my aunt, and my mother and grandmother were together. Not long after we separated, I heard on the loudspeaker that someone had fallen on the escalator. When we went to see it, my mother and grandmother had fallen. I was very frightened. They were taken to the hospital but thank God they were not seriously hurt. However, that incident traumatized me so much that it took years before I could go up or down any escalators. It took many years to get enough courage to go on an escalator. I was married, had two children, and worked at Foley's downtown when I first realized I had to conquer this fear.

With all the challenges I had to overcome during my middle school years, I finally did and was promoted to the 9th grade at Jeff Davis High School, located off Quitman Street in Houston, Texas.

HIGH SCHOOL YEARS

During my high school years, things and events in my life were becoming more challenging. I studied hard and my grades were good. I was in the Future Teachers Club there also and substituted many times. I received perfect attendance certificates, and I graduated in the upper percental of my class. However, there were events that took place in school and out that changed my life in many ways. I will try to explain.

First, at school we were confronted with Bomb Threats on a weekly basis. When that occurred everyone in the school had to leave class and walk across the street to the library and wait until we got a clear to go back in. I also remember how one student died on the field after the coach was insisting, he run the track again. One major event happened to me one day while I was in my gym class. I was the captain of my softball team, and my team was in the outfield, and I was the third baseman. The other team hit a fly ball into the field. I did not think anyone would catch it. I should not have tried but I did. I ran not looking upward and ran right into the girl that was supposed to catch the ball. I knocked her out cold. My nose was guessing blood. My opposite team came and picked me up and was taking me back inside. As I stood up, I told them that all I could see was white and I felt dizzy. I told them I would not make it. I passed out and the next thing I knew I was lying on a table in a room and the nurse was there. After that horrible lesson I never tried again to catch a ball that someone else was supposed to catch.

Another event I remember was when I had this crush on a guy on the football team. He sat by me in my home room. However, he never got the hint. However, there was Kennith who was in the ROTC, and he asked me to go with him to the school dance and again I said no.

In the meantime, at home a friend of my brother started coming by and he liked me, and we started dating. He would take me to the drive-in shows and picked me up from school every day and we would go to get a soda after school. I had asked him to take me to the prom and he said he would. However, a week before the prom was to take place, I got a call from some women who said she was his wife and that she had an investigator watching and she knew that he picked me up from school every day and she knew what and where we went each time. She begged me to stop seeing him immediately. So, when he called again, I confronted him about it, and he did not deny a thing. I then told him good-by, and I never wanted to see him again. When prom time came, I had no date. So, I decided to just go to the movies downtown by myself and I saw "The Graduate". It was good but there was standing room only. I had a lonely night.

However, things and events in my life started changing once more. Remember I told you about my older friend Diana who came to stay with her sister, Romana, who took care of the apartments across the street from me? Diana and Ramona went to Edinburg where they once lived and brought back her other sister, three brothers, and her son to live with them in the apartments. I would go over and visit with Diana and the guys started talking to me. The oldest one was name Ted, and he decided to go and fight in the Viet Nam war and unfortunately, he went missing. They have never recovered his body to this day. He was a very nice and handsome young man, and he really liked my other friend, Judy. The other two boys loved to tease me, but we became good friends. Romana's son, however, was something else. His name was Felix, and he liked me. He was a year younger than I was. He was around when I was supposed to go to my prom, but I did not ask him because I thought he was too young. However, as time went on, he and I drew closer together. On one incidence, we were playing cards in my room and the door was opened and he reach over and kissed me. Right at that moment, my father passed by, and he said, "Cut that out". I was so very embarrassed that I wanted to run away and cry, but Felix just laughed and continued to play cards with me. I soon discovered that Felix, although he was younger than I was, he was more advanced in a romantic way than I ever was. He noticed that I could not look him in the eye. He then started a game where we had to look and stare at each other and see how long one of us could do that. Of course, he always won. Another game he started was he called a kissing game when we kissed one another he would grade my kissing. As you can imagine, I never got to the A. As time went on, he even had nick names we called each other. He called me his little savage and I called him Christoper Columbus. We had a lot of fun with that.

Also, during this time in my life, I started hanging out more with my older sister, Dora Dean, who lived with us. She worked at Kelley's Restaurant and bar downtown across the street from the Rice Hotel where my father once worked.

All the wrestlers would stay at the Rice Hotel and come and eat at Kelly's and my sister would get to meet them. One day, when I was with her there, a famous champion of that day came walking down the street. She stopped him and said she wanted him to meet me. I was so afraid because he had thick black eyebrows just like my father. His name was called "Bull Curry". After he started talking, I could tell he was a nice man after all. I remember the first time my sister, Dora, took me to the wrestling matches downtown. At first, I could not see or understand why anyone would be hollowing and screaming for two people fighting but by the time it was over, I found myself doing the same thing. I started going with her more often.

It was also during this time that my sister found the love of her life. A tall dark and handsome guy came into the restaurant one day and she served him. His name was Buddy Fuller. He started coming more and more and he always had her to serve him. Then not long after, my sister announced they were getting married. They came and lived with my mother and father and me. After they were married for a few months, they got a call from the police that his three children from his ex-wife were left alone. His ex-wife suddenly passed away. They went and picked them up and they started living with all of us. There was the oldest and her name was Robbie Jean Fuller her sister, Wendy Fuller, and Ricky Fuller was the baby. We all got along fine. There was some jealousy, but we all survived. I will be discussing more about them in future chapters.

These events all took place during my high school years. That summer I got some good news that I was accepted into the Baptist University in Sharpstown.

COLLEGE YEARS

When my sister, Dora found out that I got accepted into the Baptist University she contacted my aunt Velma who worked as a secretary in Washington D.C. and ask her if there was any way she would be able to help with my college tuition. You see my sister wanted me to do what she was unable to do. I was the only child that graduated from high school and went to college in my family. She wrote back and said she could, and she did help but I also took out a loan which I eventually paid back. I remember my very first job. It was down the street from the college. I worked as a waitress in a coffee shop that my brother-in-law, Buddy was the manager. I worked there after school and on weekends for a while. Later in my second semester I started working as a waitress at Kelly's Restaurant and bar where my sister, Dora worked.

In College I met a few friends. I met this one girl. Her name was Angela, and she did not have money for lunch that day and I gladly gave her the money. She was so surprised that someone would be that nice to her. We became the best of friends. There was also another girl named Virgina who I spent the night or two with her and her grandmother and we would occasionally go to the big Baptist Church downtown. Her grandmother was in some ministry there. We three girls started our own Sorority there at the college. We had so much fun together until something unexpected happened which I will let you know later in this chapter. I remember a time when Virgina and I went on a religious retreat in Palestine Texas. There we were all spread out into groups. I was with this guy, and he was very handsome,

The idea of the group was for each other to explain one another's religion. He was of the Muslim faith, and I was of a Christian one. I tried my best to explain his and he tried his best to explain mine. We both had a lot of fun doing so. When it was time to go home, I shared with Virgina about that guy. I told her he was very handsome, and he looked like Tony Curtis the movie star. She then told some of the other girls and they told him and gave him my phone number. Not long after I returned home, I got a call from him wanting to come to see me. His name was Habib, and he was going to Texas A&M. I told him yes and gave him directions to my house. Meanwhile, Felix the next-door fellow found out about him coming. When Felix seen him over at my house, he went inside and started playing this music loudly. So loud I could hear it from across the street. He was playing "Your Cheating Heart."

I quickly took Habib inside and introduced him to my mom and dad. They liked him at first sight. I remember the first movie we ever saw together. It was "Love Bug" downtown, South Main. I remembered it well because he started telling me about how they got married over in Tunisa France where he was form. When he finished that conversation, I became very nervous because it seemed the way he was talking that he wanted to get married and that was not something I wanted just yet. Then when he brought me home the first night, he kissed me good night and it was the first time I had ever been French kissed. I thought he was going to swallow my tongue. He would come down to see me on the weekends and on one occasion, he took me to the drive-in to see another movie. He said he was going to the concession stand and get us something to drink. It took him a long time to get back and I became worried that he might have put something in my drink. I had heard of that happening to people. So, when he brought me the drink, I waited until he went out for something again and I poured it out. I am sure now that it was nothing but at that time, I was too afraid not to trust him. We went out a few more times. He bought me a beautiful Texas A&M diamond necklace. When he did ask about marriage, that is when I told him. I have always lived in the USA, and I never want to leave this nation of mine to go to France. He was very sad, but it was then we said our final goodbye.

Another important event that I recall happened after I attended a chapel service in college. Attending chapel services in the college was a requirement. This one occasion I recall very clearly. The speaker was a lady, and she told her life story about how she tried on several occasions to take her own life but every time she tried something happened to stop her. She finally found her answer was in Jesus Christ and she accepted him immediately into her heart. When I got on the bus to go home that day in 1969, I was thinking about that lady and her journey in life. A voice within me said, "Child you are going to write a book." I did not understand. I was not a Christian then. I remember saying that my life is nothing to write about. The voice then replied, "Maybe not now but later on you will". I see now how that reality came true.

It was during my college years that my brother, Glen and his wife, Alberta and their four children came to live with us. In the second semester of school, I was invited to go to Israel with a group of students from the college, but I was unable to get the funds to do so. I kept feeling that something was going to happen to me, and it did.

DECEMBER SURPRISE

It was the year 1969 and the month of December, and I remember it as if it were only yesterday. Well, you remember that young man named Felix? The one who played the music, "Your Cheating Heart" he had gone back home to his grandmother in Edinburg with the rest of the family to spend the Christmas Holidays with. I felt very lonely, but I managed to have a good Christmas after all. When he returned, he called me and asked me to come over.

I did and there was only Felix home at the time. I asked him where his mom and Diana, his aunt, were, and he told me they were out running some errands. I really did not want to be alone with him because at that moment I felt very vulnerable. I had missed him. He then began to tell me how much he missed me and that everyone down there had a partner to be with. He even spoke of a dream he had one night. He said he was sleeping outside. In those days, people could sleep outside without fear that someone would attack them. Anyway, he said he dreamed he saw me by the car, and he went and kissed me there. When he woke up, he said he felt sad and could hardly wait until he seen me again. He came over to me and started hugging and kissing me and before we knew it, we were in trouble. Somehow, I resolved in my mind that I loved him, and he was not the marring kind but that I would have something from him that nobody could ever take from me. I had no idea what I was thinking. We just got caught up in the moment and that is when we had sex. We only had it once and we both agreed to take it slowly from now on. It was very hard to do but we did it. Felix later decided to return to his grandmother. Not long after he left, I became ill. When I missed my period. I knew something was very wrong. That day, I went into the room where my sister-in-law, Alberta was, and I told her that I thought that I was pregnant. I remember her asking me what your mother would say. I told her that I did not know but that I felt somehow that this child would bring us closer as a family and he did. She told me that she and my brother, Glen, would take me to the doctor. I told her yes, I would go. She then asks me what I will do if I am pregnant. I told her that I was hoping that my sister, Wanda, who now lived in Mississippi would let me come down there and stay with them. That is when I left the room and went back into the living room. As strange as it may seem, at that exact moment the phone rang and guess who was on the other line. It was my sister, Wanda, and I was so excited that I just blurted out that I thought I may be pregnant. When she heard that she said that she could come down in the summer when school was out and pick me up. I said I would let her know when I came back from the doctor's office. She then said OK and hung up the phone.

The day did come when my brother and sister-in-law took me to the doctor's office. The test came back and sure enough I was indeed pregnant. The due date the doctor said would be September 20, 1970, and he turned out to be correct.

The days and nights following were very hard for me. I still was going to college, and I would have morning sickness so bad that I would not eat so I would not have anything in me to throw up. My classes were seemly getting harder to concentrate and more difficult as time went on. I never told my friend, Angela until I was in Mississippi, and she said I could have told her anything and she would not have judged me at all. Later I found out she got married and joined the Marines. My friend, Virgina had already moved away so I could not tell her anything about it. Felix had no idea that I was pregnant, and he had joined the Army. It was one of his uncles that finally told him about it.

During this time, another incident occurred. You remember me telling you about a fellow named Kennith? Kennith was the one in Jr High and High school that wanted to date me, and I never would. Well, he finally got his wish. One day he called me and told me that he was visiting a friend of ours from school and they were looking in the yearbook and they came across my picture and he asked her if she knew what had happened to me. She then told him where and how to get in touch with me. On our first date, I told him that I was pregnant and if he felt uneasy about that that I would understand, and we could go our separate ways. He said that he did not care because he always liked me and wanted to be with me someday. He was the one who helped me to have more confidence in myself. We went out a few times and I remember the last words he told me before I left to go to my sister's. He told me that I was going to be great and that I would come back with a beautiful baby. He said because he knew I was worried about it. I did not have to tell him. He just knew.

Before all of this, I was still waiting for the summer to come when I would be going to my sister's. During this time, I did have another job. I quit the coffee shop and started working with my sister, Dora, at Kelly's. She had no idea that I was pregnant. One day at work, I was looking at the menu for the day and this thought came across my mind that I would give my child to my sister, Dora, because she lost hers. Then a voice within said, "No. Then I ran to where my sister was and told her that she was pregnant. She looked at me and asked me How did I know? I did not tell her.

Still the only people in my family knew I was pregnant were my brother and sister-in-law and my sister, Wanda in Mississippi. In the meantime, I would ask my mother to sleep with me at night and one night my father came home late from work. He came into the room where my mother and I were sleeping and told her that Glen, my brother who worked with him at the Houston Club downtown, had said that I was pregnant. I remember she looked at me and said, "Is that the reason you are going to your sisters? "I told her yes and I thought when she found out that she would not love me anymore. She then said I will always love you and I will come down and be with you when the baby is born. For the first time in a long time, I rested peacefully.

Summer came and school was out. The day finally arrived when my sister came to pick me up. I said my goodbyes to everyone. I thought this might be the last time that I would ever see them again. I thought I might die in childbirth like my grandmother on my father's side did having her 12th child.

When I arrived at my sister's I discovered that she already had a whole drawer filled with new baby clothes. She had already bought everything I would need. I had my own room, and everything was so nice and neat in there. As time went by, I really began to miss my mother. I was never away from her for long periods of time. One night I prayed, Lord, please send my mother to me. The next day she came, and I was so happy to see her. She stayed until the baby, and I was ready to go back home.

FINDING SALVATION

After a few days at my sister's, I asked her if there was a library near her, and she said yes, there was. The next week, she took me, and I checked out a book called, *"The Power of Positive Thinking,"* by Norman Vincent Peal. When we returned home that day, a pamphlet was on the doorstep of my sister's home. I picked it up and began to read it. It said, "Salvation is available today." 2nd Corinthians 6:1 After reading that and more in the book I just picked up from the library, I went into my room, kneeled on my knees, and asked Jesus Christ to come into my heart that very day. I was then, by faith, saved in June of 1970.

From that day forward, things in my life changed. Whatever happened in life's journey from that point onward was in God's hands and not mine. From then on, my life was no longer about me; I would always be focused on His will for my life. I did not attend church there, but I began praying and reading God's word every day.

When I went to see the doctor for the first time, I knew even then that my God went before me. The doctor I chose happened to be the only one in the town who would take care of the baby and me. He was nice, but he did say that I needed to be on a rabbit's diet. When I got back into the car, I told my sister what the doctor said, and she laughed because she knew it meant for me to eat more salads. I did not see the humor in that. The next thing that the doctor told me was that every other visit, he would be drawing blood. I sure did not like that, so I was to have an appointment on September 18, 1970, and I prayed that I would not have to have my blood drawn. Guess what? When I arrived for my appointment, I was told by the receptionist that the doctor had been called out to an emergency and would not be able to see me, but his assistant would. His assistant did not require me to have my blood drawn that day. Two days later, I gave birth to my son. Before he was born, I often thought of whether the baby would be a girl or a boy and who he or she would look like. In those days, they did not have an ultrasound where you could see the sex of your baby before it was born.

So, I prayed to the Lord to know what my baby would look like. I had always wanted a blond-haired, blue-eyed boy. One night, before his birth, I had a dream. In that dream, this little boy set up, and he looked exactly like one of my sister's boys. He had blond hair and blue eyes. Of course, when I woke up, I realized it was only a dream.

FIRST CHILD

I was taken to the hospital, as I stated previously, on September 20, 1970. I remember very clearly. It was on a Sunday. The doctor came in, and he was still wearing his Sunday best. He examined me and told me that the birth would probably not be until late this evening. He then left the room. After he left, the lady next to me began screaming in pain. I felt a little guilty because I was not feeling any pain. It was just that my water had broken, and that is the reason I had to come to the hospital then. A week before, I watched Art Linkletter show that showed a pregnant woman, and he was saying that the baby will come faster if you pant like a dog. It sounded crazy, but I began. To do just that. Not long after that, the nurse came in to check me and it hurt as if you know what. My pain then started. I asked for ice chips, and the nurse brought me some.

With all the pain that I was having, I began to question God. I ask Him if I must suffer because of my sin. At that exact moment, I heard this voice within me say, "No, your sins have been forgiven."

Immediately after that the nurse came in to check on me again. I begged her not to because it hurt so bad the first time. She looked at me and said I am taking you to the delivery room right now. In the delivery room, I heard one nurse say to the other nurse that it was going to be a Britch birth. The other nurse said, "How can you tell?" The nurse replied, "Because I can see one of its feet." The next thing I remember was that I kept saying I was sorry that I was crying like a baby. My doctor replied, "Having a baby is the only time to cry." The next thing I remember was the doctor hit his head on the big light above me and blurted out not-so-nice words. I said again, "I was sorry." Then he told me to start counting to 10 backwards. I got as far as 7, and I was out. So, again, on September 20, 1970, I gave birth to a 6-pound and 7-ounce baby boy. I named him Michael Aundre' after one of the history men I learned about when I attended college. The doctor and nurse came in and told me that I did a great job in the delivery room, but I never understood what they meant. Also, the doctor told me that it was touch and go, but thanks to God, we were able to get him out without me having a cesarean operation. He said if he was one pound more, he would have had to perform the cesarean operation.

Then he informed me that if I had him by cesarean, all future births would have to be done by cesarean.

The next thing I remember was when the doctor and nurse came in to examine me later that day. They looked and laughed and said, "Her hemorrhoids were worse than her stitches." I sure did not see any humor in that.

Now, I had heard that you cannot be released from the hospital until you have at least one bowel movement, so I begin to pray for that. I did because it felt like they had sewed me all up. God did answer my prayer.

When they brought my baby boy to me, I could not believe my eyes. He was very handsome and had blond hair and blue eyes He looked just like one of my sister's boys, just like in my dream. I still question if he was really mine because his father was Spanish, with dark hair and brown eyes. I told them that maybe he belonged to the lady next to me. That is when they said, "No, she had a baby girl."

Later, I found out that she could not see her baby yet because she was born with R.H. negative blood and that the doctor hoped that this light that they put under her would work. They told her that there was a real possibility that it would not work, and they would have to do more invasive procedures. At that moment, I remembered what the voice within me had said, "Child, you will help someone." I began to pray hard for this situation. Within a matter of hours, the doctor came in and said to the lady, "I cannot believe my eyes, but your little girl is doing great, and the light we put under her really worked. Now, the nurse will bring in your little girl to meet you."

Another memory there was when two nurses came into the room; one was a woman, and one was a male. They asked us if we wanted to take a sponge bath. The female nurse went over to the lady, and I thought in my mind that no man was going to give me a sponge bath. I asked him if I could take a shower. He took me down to take a shower. I got in, and as I was coming out of the shower, everything began turning white, like what happened to me in High school. I decided then I would never do that again. However, the next day came, and I was released from the hospital, so I did not have to take any more showers there.

I was so glad to be back home with my baby boy, Michael. Both my mother and sister were there to help me. Not long after being home, I found myself lying in bed with my legs apart in pain, watching the T.V. from the other room. I remembered the vision I had seen before I went to the hospital to have my baby. The vision of seeing myself in my room, legs apart and watching the T.V. from the next room. Now, the vision came to pass. I was in so much pain that I prayed that Michael would start crying and wake up my mother so she could put the medicine for my stitches on. Michael started crying, and my mother woke up, and she did apply the medicine. The next day, I remember walking to take a bath with my legs apart. I got into the tub, and I began to pray, "Father God, I need healing. I sold my T.V. to pay the doctor's bill, and my sister paid the hospital bill. I do not want her to have to pay anymore if I must go back to the doctor." The voice within said, "Medicine." That is all the voice said. I got out and dressed and walked the same way I came, and I heard my sister talking on the phone to my doctor. After she got off, she said the doctor was sending over a bottle of medicine because he thought that I might have been allergic to the medicine that was prescribed for the stitches. He also said that if this medicine does not work within 24 hours, to take her to the E.R. right away, for that meant blood poisoning had occurred. I then told my mother that I just wanted to lie down and not apply the medicine at the time. Later that afternoon, the new medicine that the doctor had ordered arrived. I asked my mother and sister to pray with me, and we prayed that this bottle of medicine would be a miracle. Within a few hours, the infection came pouring out. I could bring my legs back together, and I experienced no more pain. It was a miracle for me. Not long after that, I was able to go back to my home in Houston, Texas.

When I got home, I realized I had to find a full-time job. I was determined to pay my sister back for the hospital bill that she paid for. I began working at Big Seven Food Market off North Main near my home.

RETURNING HOME

As I indicated before, when I got home from the hospital, I started working my first full-time job at The Big Seven Food Market off North Main in Houston, Texas. After returning home from my sister's, I got a call from a very sweet gentleman whose name was Kennith, the one from school. He asked me how I was doing and if I would like to go and have lunch with him. I agreed, and we started dating again. Then, after several months, I got a call from another very sweet, handsome young man whose name was Felix, the father of my baby boy. He had told me that he had joined the army but that he was the only son, and his uncle had been missing in the Vietnam War, so he was exempt. He was calling me because he had just found out that I was pregnant and gave birth to his son. He said his uncle Tommy told him. He asks me why I never said anything to him about the pregnancy. I told him that I did not think he was the marrying kind and that I would raise him on my own. He asked to talk to my father, and at that point, I do not recall that conversation, but I do remember Felix coming back on the line, and he asked me to marry him. I said, "Yes, I will marry you." He told me that he would be coming down next week and we could get married then. On the very day that Felix was to come, the phone rang, and Kennith was on the other line, and he wanted to come over and get his music player that I had borrowed. I was planning to tell him about Felix over the phone. I know that was not too kind, but I was a coward. I never have had to break someone's heart like that. I had to, though, because Felix was already there waiting to see me at Jack in the Box on the corner. So, when Kennith arrived, I went inside and got his music player. We sat in his car and talked. He asked how I was doing and said, "Did I not tell you that you will come back with a beautiful baby?"

That is when I had to tell him that the baby's father had called me and wanted to get married and help me raise our son together. I could barely look him in the eye because I knew how much that hurt him. With tears in his eyes, he said, "All I ever wanted for you was to be happy. If raising your son with his father makes you happy, then that is all I need." We hugged each other, and we said our goodbyes.

After Kennith left, I walked to Jack in the Box and met Felix. It felt wonderful seeing him again. We hugged and kissed each other. Then we left and came home. We were out on the porch, and it was already night. I could tell by his actions that he wanted to get interment with me. He kept hugging and kissing me. It was hard for me as well. I felt very vulnerable at that moment. He asks, "Do you want to walk down to the school like we used too long ago?" I said, "I would." So, when we got there, Felix began hugging and kissing me again. I knew then what he wanted from me. Again, it was very hard to refrain from doing so, for I loved him and missed him greatly. But now I was different. I then told him not to laugh at me because I found Jesus as my personal Savior, and I could not do this until we got married. He just looked at me and said, "Baby, I am not laughing, and I do respect your wishes." The next day, we got our marriage license, and we were getting married at the Justice of the Peace downtown. Meanwhile, another tragic event took place at home.

If you recall my sister Dora and her husband Buddy and their three children lived with us. At this point, I need to give you some background on what happened before Buddy got sick. If you recall, Dora, my older sister, lost a baby, and I was not there for the funeral. I felt afterwards that, somehow, she would have another baby that would live. That day did come, and she gave birth to a baby girl. She was born in November of 1970, two months after my boy. They named her Dorie Fuller after her mother. Not long after she was born, the doctor discovered that she had R.H. negative blood and that they would need to completely drain her blood and put in new. I guess in those days they did not use the special kind of light that was used on the baby when I was in hospital having mine. During this time, the doctor did not want my sister to know because of her heart. So, Buddy asked me if I would go with him to witness and be an encouragement for him. I told him I would. He kept praising Dora for all that was going on. The first blood transfusion did not work. The doctor called Buddy and told him we needed to do this again. Again, I went with him. The doctor also told him that he might have to do it a third time but that he really did not want to. At that time, Buddy's oldest daughter, Robbie, was there with me. I asked her if she would go with me to the chapel, and she said, "Yes, I will go with you." When we got into the chapel and prayed, I looked up and saw there was a huge bible opened on a stand. I got up and looked at it. The scripture I remember to this day is Ecclesiastes 1: 14:

> *"I have seen all the works that are done under the sun; and behold, all is vanity and vexation of spirit."*

I then looked up the meaning of vanity in a dictionary, and it is an excessive pride in one's appearance, qualities, abilities, achievements, etc. I was praying for an answer as to why all this was happening to the child that God told me would be born alive this time. After reading this, I turned to Robbie and told her that I knew what the problem was. Buddy had been giving all the credit to my sister instead of giving it to the Almighty God. She then realized that I could hear from God. We prayed and returned and found out that this time, the transfusion worked, and there would be no more done. Both Dora and Dorie came home that day. Everything seemed to be going well until Christmas Eve night. As a tradition of ours, when my father came home from work on Christmas Eve, we always opened our presents. The Christmas Eve of 1970 turned out wrong. Buddy had been working with my father at the Houston Club downtown at night, and this night was no different.

However, when Buddy arrived, he was drunk and fell on the porch. I was very upset because I knew we would not be opening our presents that night. In private, I just raised my hands up to God and said, "Father God, if a child cannot change him, then you take over, for I am done." Six months later, Buddy became very ill. He went to Ben Taub Hospital and was admitted. The doctors could not find out what was wrong with him. Finally, one doctor said it was cancer and gave him a short time to live. Our pastor, Pastor A. L. Gatlin went to see Buddy in the hospital. I do not recall any conversation they might have had. But when I found out, I began to pray and ask forgiveness for giving up on him, and the voice within me said, "He will not die" I believed it. However, I thought at the time that God meant it physically and not spiritually. When Buddy got home, our pastor, Brother Gatlin, came to visit him. That next day was one of the most horrible days of my life because Buddy did die.

Now, just imagine this: I have my future husband in the house with me, and my sister came in and asked me to go with her to the hospital to take Buddy because he was very sick. I told her I would. She came back within minutes and said, "Nethermind, Buddy is dead." I could not believe it. I had to see it for myself. I ran into the room, and he was stiff and lying on the bed. It was true. He was indeed dead. I ran back into the other room screaming this cannot be because the Lord told me He would not die. I kept raving on, and Felix had to slap me to bring me to reality again.

However, the next morning was horrible. I had to face Robbie, who I had told her that the Lord had said that her father would not die. I remember well what happened next. I was going to the bathroom, and I saw her raising the oven door to put a roast in for dinner. My eyes met hers, and I could not say a word. I did not understand the betrayal of God at that point. However, after just a few moments, Robbie and I went into the living room, but still, I had nothing to say. At that time, Sister Gatlin, the pastor's wife, came in and sat down in our rocking chair, and I asked her when Pastor Gatlin spoke to Buddy yesterday if he had told her anything that Buddy might have said. She said with much excitement in her voice, "My husband, I have never seen him like this before." He said he had to get to Buddy and talk about his soul. He said that Buddy told him the only thing he regrets is that he had nothing to leave his family. My husband then told him you can leave them with peace of mind knowing that you are saved and on your way to Heaven. She said that Buddy told her husband that he did not know it was that simple. At that moment, Robbie and I looked at each other and smiled. We knew then that Buddy did die, but he lives now in eternity. After all this, I asked my sister if she thought it would still be ok for Felix and I to get married that day. She informed me that Buddy would have it no other way.

MARRIAGE AND DIVORCE

So, on March 5, 1971, Felix and I went down to the courthouse downtown and got married. A strange event happened shortly after. I should have taken it as an omen at the time. As we started walking down the street, a huge wind came up, and our marriage license flew out of my hand and landed under a bus. Of course, when the bus left, Felix picked it up. However, the damage had begun. We lived with my mother and father. One night, Felix came in, and he was drunk. He immediately laid down on the bed, and when I turned him over, I saw in my mind that it was not Felix but Buddy's face. I immediately ran out the back door and screamed Lord, "I can't do your work anymore. I can't write the book you want me to." At that moment, I heard the voice within say one word, "Michael". I knew at that instance what the Lord wanted me to do, and that was to take care of my son, Michael. I came to my senses and went inside. I went to bed, and the next morning, Felix said he could not find any work here, and he wanted to take us to live with his grandmother in Edinburgh. I was still working here and making a living. I wanted stability for my son, and I was not sure that Felix could do that at this time. I told him I could not go but that I would stay here and take care of Michael until he was able to get a job to send for us to come and live with him there. That never happened. I assume he found someone else to be with. I never heard from him again until he came back down, and I filed for a divorce on October 18, 1971. We were married only seven months and had known each other for several years. I will discuss Felix again in a future chapter.

TRAGIC EVENT

While still working at Big Seven, a tragic event happened. I met this guy from a friend of mine, and I thought he would be a nice person to be with. His name was George. However, I discovered that I was wrong. Now, since Felix and I divorced, I did not see any sense in taking birth control pills any longer, so I stopped taking them, but it was in the middle of my cycle, and I started bleeding. That is when I decided to start taking them again. I believe that God was leading me, and he knew what was going to happen. Several months went by, and George came over to my house and asked me how long my husband and I had been divorced. I knew what he was getting at. I told him it had been a good while since I had relations with my husband. He then said no more about it. I remember it was a Sunday night, and he called me and asked if I would like to go riding in his new car with him and some of his friends. I did not think any harm would come, so I agreed to go. He drove down the main street and pulled into this big house, and I remember it was right next to a flower shop. He told me that his father wanted to meet me. We walked inside. The door was left open, and he turned the T.V. on. Then he left the room, and I thought he was going to get his father.

However, he came back with a smile on his face. He closed and locked the front door. I asked him where his father was, and he would not answer. He just went over and turned off the T.V. He turned off the lights, and then he came and literally picked me up from the couch. I was frightened and kept telling him no, that I wanted to go home now. He proceeded to place me on the bed. I knew then there would be no stopping him. I prayed, "Father God help me." A voice within said, "Child, be still and know that I am your God." So, I obeyed, and I stayed still until he was through. Afterward, he apologized and said that I was telling the truth and that I had not had relations for a long time. He then said that I did not have to worry about his friends coming in and that he was the only one who would touch me in that manner. I told him that I accepted his apology, but that God knew it would happen, and because I was still on birth control, it prevented an unwanted pregnancy. Thank you, Jesus. The following day, he had the nerve to try to talk to me. I told him that I never wanted to see him again, and I never did.

I continued working at Big Seven. One day, while I was checking out this couple, they left a $30.00 food stamp book. At first, the enemy had me thinking I could just keep it and that no one would find out. But that thought only lasted a second. I vowed to God that when I came back from lunch and saw that couple again, I would give them their $30.00 food stamp book back. When I returned from lunch, my boss sent me to the drugs department to run the cash register there. When I looked up, I saw that same couple down one aisle. I left the register and immediately returned their food stamp book to them. They thanked me, and I returned to the drug register. Then, something very strange took place. A voice within me said for me to save $30.00 back, to pay on the only credit card I had at that time, my W. T. Grant. The same department store where my mother and grandmother had the accident on the escalator. I thought that was strange, but I obeyed, and then I discovered why. The manager came to me and told me he had to lay me off because business was too slow right now. Can you guess how long I was out of a job? I was out of a job for exactly three months, and I never had to miss my credit card payment because I obeyed the Lord. After three months, I went downtown asking the Lord everywhere I went, "Lord, do you want me here?" But I kept thinking that when I got home, someone I knew would have a job for me. I thought at first that I was going crazy thinking such a thing.

However, when I returned home that day, the phone rang, and it was an old friend of mine who said that there was a job opening where she worked at Piggly Wiggle Store as a cashier. I went and applied and was hired. One day, this handsome guy came in, and I checked him out. I never had a real conversation with him, but he would always have me check him out. The other girls told me that he really liked me. I told them they were wrong. One day, I was out on a break, and when I returned, the girls told me that the guy had come in and he was asking for me. The girls said that I was on a break and would be returning soon. He said that he would come back later to see me. He came back that evening and asked me If I would like to go and see a movie with him. His name was Mike, and he was a truck driver by trade. I reluctantly said I would. It was a good movie, but I cannot recall the name of it. The next few times we went out, I felt at ease. I told him about George and what he did, and he said that he was sorry for what happened to me.

The next evening, he came to the house to meet my mother and father and my son, Michael. It was a very pleasant visit. After a few more dates, he asked if I would like to go to his apartment and listen to some music with him. I said, "Yes, I will." He was such a gentleman and opened the door real wide. We walked inside, and he said you do not have to worry because I will not hurt you like you were hurt before. We both sat on the floor and listened to his music. It felt so right that I allowed him to hug and kiss me. I felt very safe and comfortable with him. He had no T.V., but I really enjoyed listening to his music with him. Then the following weekend, he told me that he had borrowed a friend's T.V. so we could watch it together. When we got to his apartment, he seemed very quiet. He said that I looked tired and for me to lie down on the couch but not to worry. He sat on a chair across from me. Not long after, he got up and said that he thought it was best if he took me home because he knew I had worked extra hours that day. I agreed. The ride home seemed quiet until he started telling me that he needed more in a relationship, but he never wanted to change me for anything. He said that I was too good for him. I knew then he was breaking up with me. Before he opened the door to let me out, he wanted to kiss me goodbye. I could not do that. I was so hurt that I just went to my room and cried. Now I know how Kenneth must have felt. I began to pray, "Father God, just send me someone who loves you half as much as I do." In Jesus's Name, Amen.

SECOND MARRIAGE

Not long after the breakup, I resigned from Piggly Wriggle and was re-hired at Big Seven in January 1973. Within a few weeks, an incident that would change my life again forever occurred. I was placed working at the old register because I was the only one there that knew how. That day, I was very busy. Guess who came walking in the door? It was none other than Felix and he came to tell me that he had found out that I was now a free woman. Our divorce was final. I said OK and continued to work. The next person that came through the door was a very handsome young man who said, "Hey Babe, where is the ice?" I said in a sarcastic way that it was over there. I was very busy and did not have time to chit-chat. He then said, "How come a pretty thing like you is not married yet?" To hopefully shut him up, I replied, "I was married and got a divorce. I believe then he took the hint that I was too busy to talk. He got his ice, paid the other cashier, and came back and said, "I will come to see you again. He then left. The next day I was not due for work until 3:00 p.m. At around noon time, my mother and I were playing with my son, Michael. When I caught a glance from the window of some guy coming to our fence, I looked, and it was that guy who talked to me about wanting to buy ice. I told my mother that there was a boy out there who had come to see me. She quickly grabbed Michael and said she was going to the back room. He came in looking like the rime stone cowboy. He had on a gold and white shirt, blue jeans, boots, a hat, and a gold tie. I could not believe my eyes. He came in and asked me if I would like to go and get some lunch at the Pig Stand before I go to work. I told him that would be fine. When we got to the restaurant, I asked him how in the world he knew where I lived. He said one of the cashiers told him that I was scheduled to come in at 3:00 p.m. today and gave me your address. Well, I said, "I must thank her," and I laughed. He asked me what kind of music I liked the most, and I told him, country. He said that was great because he wanted to take me dancing at the Stampede off Westheimer in Houston, Texas. He said that I would enjoy it very much. He asked if I had ever been there before, and I said no. The evening did arrive when he took me there. At first, we just sat at a table and talked. He said that he used to smoke and drink but that he quit them now. Then suddenly, he lowered his head a little and was very quiet. I was shy, so I just kept quiet. After some minutes, he stood up and asked if I wanted to dance, and I said yes. We got up and were dancing a slow dance when he whispered in my ear something I would never have dreamed of. He asked if I had ever known someone that has had seizures, and I said no then said that he had them. The only type of seizure that I could think of was the kind in which they became unconscious and could swallow their tongue. I immediately started praying within, "Father God, please do not let him have a seizure while we are here." I found out later that when he lowered his head, he had one. On the way home, I told him that God could heal him of his seizures. We begin dating on a regular basis. He would come to my house, and I would go to his. Both my mother and father liked him. When I told my father about his seizures, he told me to watch out that he would usually have one when there was a full moon. I asked him how he knew that, and he told me that he had them before. I was shocked. I never knew that about my father until then. One funny and strange thing happened while we were at the Stampede one evening. Both Billy and I left the dance floor and went into the room where the pool table was. He wanted to show me it because he said that he loved to play pool. But this time, we were just sitting on the side and talking. I do not know why I asked him this. I asked him what he would do if his ex-wife were here at the same time we were. He said, "I do not know, but it could happen." Well, after that, we went into the ballroom to dance, and while we were dancing, Billy whispered in my ear, "Do not look now, but my ex-wife is here." I thought oh, that was just great. However, she did not see us, and we left right then.

That next day, I had gone over to his house to see him. He wanted to show me something. He went into his room and brought out some rings. He told me that this belonged to his ex-wife. I thought this guy wanted to get married. I better get out of here quickly. However, I stayed. He said that his mom and dad had gone to the laundry mat, and they would be gone for a while. He started hugging me, and I told him I had powers, but he just laughed. Right then, his phone rang in his room. He went to answer it. He came back and said that it was funny because that had never happened before. I said again, "I got powers." He just continued to kiss me, and his phone rang again. And again, there was no one on the line. He started once again to hug and kiss me, and suddenly, his parents knocked on the door. He then just laughed.

In a joking manner, he said, "I guess you do have powers after all."

Several weeks later, at the Stampede, Billy begins talking to me about marriage. He told me that he did not want to get married until we saw each other's temper. I thought that was strange, but I agreed.

However, we got married, and then I saw his temper, which really scared me. One evening, his friend Richard took Billy and me dancing at the Stampede and something really went wrong. We had been dancing for quite some time when I asked Billy to ask Richard, his friend, to take us home. I had to get up early for work the next morning. He said he would, but he kept putting it off. I ask him again and again. The third was too much for him. He just broke away from me and kicked a chair, and several more fell at the same time. I was so embarrassed that I just wanted to get out of there as quickly as possible.

Billy and I dated for six months, and then he asked me to marry him. I said, "Yes." We were married on June 28, 1973. We were married by Reverend A. L. Gatlin at Bethel Pentecostal Church of God, which was my home church, and it became Billy's as well. Reverend Gatlin was one of a kind. I was told that he lost a finger while building the church. He buried it under the rubble and kept on building the church. There will be more discussion about the church later.

From this point forward, it will be very difficult to cover all the events that occurred in my life after I married my husband, Billy Cross. However, I will try my best to cover most events that will give my God the glory. I was married to him for 48 wonderful years. So, I hope you can understand how difficult it would be for me to cram that many years of life on paper.

After we got married, Billy, my son Michael, and I lived in a duplex not too far from my husband's mom and dad.

After resigning from Big Seven, I went to work at Austral Oil Company, where Billy's sister was working. Her boss was an Attorney there and Billy hired him for a legal adoption of Michael, from that day on, Michael became our son. Billy was the only father that Michael ever knew. They both bonded very well together. Not long after we got married, Felix came to see me. he wanted to get back together with me, but I told him that I was happy and that I had married a very good man. He said whatever I do, I must refrain from saying anything negative concerning him. He said just let him find that out for himself. To this day I have kept my promise and never said anything negative about him. Before Felix left that day he said to me, "If you are happy, then I am happy for you." Then he said, "Goodbye."

I never told Billy that he even came by as I felt it was not that important

MORE WORKING YEARS

When Michael was about five, both Billy and I were working at The Texas Children's Hospital downtown in the Medical Center. I was a special accounts biller, and he worked in the dispensary, taking the medications to the operating rooms. Everything seemed to be going well until a heavy burden came over me. That day, I went to the chapel on my break and prayed.

After I prayed, I felt the Lord wanted me to resign from the hospital. When I returned, it looked like the very date on my calendar was marked. I immediately went to my supervisor and gave two weeks' notice.

Afterward, I became worried. I forgot that Billy had just started his job, and we had a child to take care of as well. I had my doubts. Then I felt like I heard from God that if you do not want extravagant things, everything will work out. I believed in God, and everything worked out for us until my sweet, loving husband decided we needed a larger TV and some new furniture.

A week later, I went to apply with an agency downtown. When I got there, I went in to talk to the lady and in the middle of our conversation, I almost started crying. I told her that I felt like I should not be there but at the hospital where my mother was. I told her I must leave, and I apologized.

However, on my way home, I kept feeling that I was going to hear about a job. Sure enough, when I got home, the phone rang, and it was the same agency, and she said a company named Gulf Warehouse was looking for a person who worked with different accounts. She told me his name and gave me the address and phone number.

His name was Mr. Wallace, and he was very nice. The thing that sold me was he said, "God had led him there." That was all it took for me. I was hired and began working with his wife and several others in the office.

About three weeks later, I was talking to my husband on the phone, and he said in a very harsh tone. "What is this bill for $300.00 from this agency?" I said, "I thought this was a prepaid fee." I told him that I would take care of it. I looked around and did not see anyone in the office. I started thinking that if I went into Mr. Wallace's office and told him that if fired me, he would not have to pay the fee, and neither would I. The other workers had returned, and I, on my break, went to talk to Mr. Wallace. I shyly stood at the door and said, "Mr.

Wallace, there has been a mistake made." He said with a stern voice, "There sure has." I figured at this point that he must have seen his bill for the fee. When I told him what I suggested, he said that he spoke with all the workers there and they all liked my work. He said, "We do not want you to leave. Besides all that, God told me to pay the fee." God did used me while I was working there. There was a gentleman working there who was an atheist. I began talking to him about the bible, and one day, he accepted Jesus Christ into his heart. I continued working, and yes, we got the larger TV and the new furniture my husband had wanted.

Two weeks later, my husband resigned from the hospital and was eagerly looking for another job. Michael was in kindergarten at Robert E. Lee at the time, the same elementary school that both Billy and I went to.

One day, he came running home and said, "Daddy, they need a custodian at my school." Billy had been praying to find a job, and when he heard Michael, he said, "That is my job." He went to apply the next day. He had a seizure during the interview, but somehow God gave him favor, and he was hired. He worked for HISD for 26 years and then he retired in 2001.

I continued working at Gulf Warehouse until something happened. I remember when I was working at the hospital, I went to the chapel and prayed that God would teach me His love. One night, while my husband was in the living room listening to records, and I was lying on my bed, the voice of the Lord said, "You are going to have a child. You are to name her Mary Martha." After I heard that, I thought that I must be going crazy here because I was on birth control, and I was not going to get off it.

Seven weeks later, I was with my son, who was getting his shots for school. While there, someone had passed out a pamphlet concerning birth control. It read that it causes too much sugar in your system, which may cause your legs to feel heavy at times. I had no idea that this was a warning from God until I tried to go back on them.

So, I made up my mind, and I prayed, "Father God, whichever comes first, a baby or owning our own home." I did not think we would ever own a home because we had no credit. I should have known better because, with God, all things are possible.

It did happen. First was the baby. She was born on June 1, 1977. Her name, though, was Kimberly. We did not name her as the Lord told me because Billy and my mother-in-law said that they were two first names. My husband then said, "Let's name her Kimberely after your name." All through school, I called myself Emily because I thought the name Emma was too old-fashioned.

After resigning from Gulf Warehouse, I started working at Foley's Department Store downtown. I worked there as an account biller. I worked for several years, and then I resigned and began working for Gulf Oil, which later became Chevron USA. I worked there for thirteen years and took a temporary retirement.

Then, I started working at Kelly's Services, all of which my assignments were full time at ExxonMobil for another thirteen years. Taking a break from Kelly's Services, I worked as a teacher in two Christian Schools in Houston, Aldine Christian Academy and Champions Christian Academy in Houston, Texas, for several years. I finally retired in 2016.

SECOND CHILD

To be perfectly honest with you, my second child was a handful. What I meant about that was she was a very strong-willed little girl. I see now why the Lord wanted me to name her Mary Martha. It was like she had two different personalities. While the first one exhibited kindness to others, the second displayed selfish behavior.

However, one thing I did know was that she loved her brother from the get-go. She knew he would always protect her. Whenever she was punished, he would always take her side, and she was aware of that. The other person she always knew would be on her side was her grandmother, Billy's mother. She took care of her from birth until we moved, and then she felt she had only her brother.

My mother, her grandmother, passed away in 1978, and my father, her grandfather, passed away in 1979. So, she just had Billy's mom and dad as her grandparents.

One day, she was talking to her school counselor, and she told him that she heard that her big brother, Michael, was leaving to join the Army and that she would miss him a lot. The next day, the counselor called me and told me to comfort her about her brother's leaving because he felt that she would start acting out after he left. She did. She had separation anxiety when her brother left. She started having a lot of trouble in school. We had her tested, and she was diagnosed with attention deficit hyperactivity disorder (ADHD). It was a learning problem she struggled to overcome throughout her schooling years due to a lack of awareness about the disorder. She started acting out, causing her to hang out with the wrong type of people.

I remember when she was young, she was very curious about everything. I still recall when one day, we were over Billy's mom and dad visiting, and Billy fixed a cup of hot coffee and left it on the corner of the table. He went to close the back door. I was in the kitchen at the time, and I failed to notice that she had reached up to see what was in the cup, and it had spilled on her.

I immediately pulled her shirt off and applied medicine. The burn looked bad. Billy and I both knew we would have to take her to the ER. Before we left, we prayed. The doctor at the ER told us it was a good thing that we brought her there. She had a third-degree burn, and he said that she would have a scar for the rest of her life. When we got back home, Billy and I prayed again, and within two weeks, her scar was gone.

She was truly a miracle that God sent to us.

After she was born, I heard the Lord say to me, "It shall be Kimberly. For her seed shall come before me." I did not understand what that meant unless it was concerning the four children that she gave birth to. She gave me four beautiful grandchildren, David Kane, Destiny Kolene, Daniel, and Brendon. They are all grown now and living their own lives. I am very proud of all of them.

Also, while I was in the hospital giving birth to her, there was a young lady next to me, and she heard me praying, and she wanted to get saved. I called for the Chaplin, and he came, and she accepted Jesus Christ into her heart that day. The funny thing was she was five days early and I was five days late in giving birth to our girl. Before giving birth, the Lord spoke to me and told me that I would be of help to someone again this time when I went into the hospital to have my baby. It all came to pass then.

Moreover, the most lasting memory that I have of my second child, Kimberly, was the dedication she showed to taking care of her father, my husband, Billy, in the last stages of his life. In her earlier years, she took a nursing aide class, and she did not realize how God would use that to help her father.

During those painful days, she would help bathe him, fix special food, and even change his diapers. And when the doctors put him in hospice and he was sent home with oxygen, she stayed by his bedside, administered his medicine, and cared for him throughout the night. It was something I was unable to do since I had caught Covid and was unable to get out of bed until the next morning when he passed away.

Kimberly is doing much better now. She is getting the professional help that she needs to cope. Whenever I get to talk with her, she sounds much more confident, and she has built a firm trust in God.

As of now, I just want to say that I am thankful to God for blessing me with my second child, Kimberly. Although we had our differences from time to time, we always found a way back to reconcile and love each other. She truly became a miracle sent by God.

THE FIRE

We were still living in the duplex downstairs next to Billy's mom and dad. However, they had brought a new home and had moved away. One day, I decided that we would all go to town and look at the furniture that I wanted to buy for the house.

When we boarded the bus, all four of us, Billy, Michael, Kimberly and me, sat at the back. Kimberly was just a small baby at the time. As soon as we settled down in our seats, I had a vision where I saw that when I went to the door to get off the bus, the door closed. I did not know why I had such a vision, until I got up to get off the bus.

Billy got off first, followed by Michael holding the stroller. Finally, when I proceeded to step out carrying little Kimberly in my arms, the vision materialized. But thanks to God, He had already provided the miracle that I fell on one knee instead of tripping over while stepping out of the bus. I managed to protect my baby by holding on to her real tight.

The bus driver stopped the bus and came to check on me. He thought we got hurt badly. He asked me if I needed help, but I refused and told him the baby and I was fine.

When we got halfway home, my son, Michael, insisted that he walk ahead of us to go home. It was just a few blocks, and we could see him, so I did not mind. He was about a block when he began screaming, "There is a fire truck at our house, and I can see grandma and grandpa there." Do not ask me why, but at that moment, I just said, "Thank you, Lord," for some reason.

When we arrived, we discovered that our front door had been broken. We went inside, and there was the smell of smoke all over everything. The firemen told us that the people upstairs had left an iron on, and it started burning. I was very thankful that we had no real damage except the smoke.

After the Firemen left, Billy's mom and dad insisted that we come and stay with them, so we did. We packed some clothes for all of us and went to their house. Later, we got the rest of our furniture and things, and we stored them in his parent's garage. We had been living with them for several months when I heard again from the Lord, and he said, "Child, I want you to save up $1000.00 for a home." I had been praying for a home for a long time now.

Not long after that, my husband, Billy, was bleeding with his hemorrhoids badly. He was scheduled to go to the doctor the next day. His mother was going with him since I was still working.

However, in the middle of the night, the Lord told me to go instead, so I obeyed. After the doctor examined him, he told us that he would need an operation, and that the co-pay would be $1000.00. Billy told me no, that the Lord had told us to save that for a home.

I told him we would try another hospital, and we did, but we were told the same thing. I then became a little uneasy, thinking that if I did not allow him to get this done, I would be blamed if anything happened to him. I told Billy, "Honey, let's get this done." He said no and that he was going to trust God.

In the meantime, I had already told our realtor to stop searching for a home for us because I would not have the funds for the down payment because of a medical emergency that occurred with my husband.

However, somehow, she called soon after and said there was a home that she really wanted us to look at, and she thought it would be perfect for us. I told my husband that I had to work, but if he and his mom wanted to see it and liked it, then I knew I would, too.

The next day, both told me they really liked the home. That weekend, I went to see it for myself, and I really liked it also. We got together with the realtor, and she said the down payment would be $1000.00, and we agreed. We were accepted into a mortgage company. And not long after that, we moved into our very first home.

FIRST HOME

Not long after we moved in, we found out that the previous owner was a retired preacher. After hearing that, I felt blessed to be in my new home. I loved it there, and I met some nice neighbors. Sharon, her father, and her two girls, Serena and Connie, became very good friends with my daughter as well. Her father took us anywhere we needed to go.

You see, Billy's license was denied because of seizures. I was too afraid to drive because a long time ago, in my dad's brand-new dart, I had a small accident. So, Billy and I had to depend on other people for eight years of our marriage. I finally did get enough courage to get my license.

Then, after Billy was seizure-free for two years, he was able to get his license back. We rode the bus back and forth to work. Many good and bad events took place living in my first home. However, in all of them, I felt the presence of the Lord. I would like to share my good memories there first. Our next-door neighbor had a small child whose name was Lisa, and she was the same age as my little girl, and my daughter invited her to go to Sunday School with us. I was the Sunday school teacher, and one day, she accepted Jesus Christ into her heart. Today, she is still happily on fire for the Lord. I am very proud of her.

Another event that I recall that had the Lord's hand in was one Saturday when it rained hard. Amid the heavy downpour, my husband and I both noticed that water was leaking badly from our roof. We did not know what to do, since it was late in the evening, we were unable to call anyone.

We got down on our knees and prayed that our roof would not fall upon us. By early Sunday morning, we heard something on top of our roof did not know what it was. So, we went out to see. discovered that it was our dear church friend up on our roof. We did not know how he knew about it. We never contacted him regarding our dilemma. When Brother Eddy came down from the roof, he explained.

He told us that in the middle of the night, the Lord had told him to get to the Crosses fast; their roof was about to collapse. He fixed our roof that day, and we thanked him for doing so. After he left, Billy and I knelt in prayer to thank the Lord for sending Brother Eddy to help us.

Another memory in my first home involved losing $1000.00. To explain this, I must give you some background. My father, who had passed, had a two-story home that my uncle bought, and my uncle had distributed its share between us children. I was given $1000.00 for my share. I Had some new furniture on layaway, and I was supposed to pay the $1000.00 to finish off my balance. I had the cash in an envelope, along with my tithes and a few Astro World coupons. After church, I reach into the envelope to give the youth pastor the coupons.

I got home, and I looked for the envelope, which I believed had my $1000.00 in it. I could not find the money. I began to panic, and Billy was taking a nap, so I sure did not want to tell him. He would have been furious with me.

At first, I was going to call my mother-in-law because she was sitting next to me and ask her if she had seen the envelope. But then I thought I did not want her to think our church people would ever take something like that. After that thought came a voice within that said, "Child, the steps of a righteous man are ordered by the Lord." I knew that was scripture. But I ask from within, "Then surely I must have taken the wrong steps somehow."

After that, I thought, "Well, I have a key to the church because we were the custodians." So, I asked Sharon and her husband if they wouldn't mind taking me back to the church. I never woke my husband up to tell him where I was going. He needed to rest anyway.

As soon as I got into the church, I ran to the pew where I was sitting and picked up the envelope, but it was empty. I ran down to the altar and began to cry out to God. "Oh, God, where are you?" I heard this voice within say, "I am right here." I got up from my knees and immediately called my pastor, Pastor Gary Cox, and asked him if anyone had told him about this money, and he said no. He told me that he would be praying for me. Pastor Cox would always come and get us for church, for if you remember, I told you that my husband and I did not have our license yet.

I was so grateful that when the pastor picked us up that Sunday night, he did not mention my situation because I really did not want Billy to find out if it was possible. That night at church, Pastor Cox announced that someone there still had the victory even with what she was going through. I was grateful once more because he never mentioned my name.

That night, when we returned home, I told my husband that I did not feel like eating and that I just wanted to fast and pray. I went into our room to kneel and pray, but something just drove me to my calculator case, and there I found the

$1000.00. I was so happy, and then I remembered I had separated that money from my tithes. Then the scripture came back. "The steps of a righteous man are ordered of the Lord." Psalms 37:23-24. I never told Billy.

Another memory I recall was when I was out of work and in need of a job. I prayed to the Lord to send me where he wanted me to work. The next day, I was offered not one job but two. I chose Gulf Oil at that time. God Bless me greatly there. I worked there for many years. When I first worked there, I had this boss who would cuss with every word, and when I started working for him closely, he saw how my character was, and for some reason, he did not cuss anymore. We became the best of friends. One day, I went into his office and said, "Mr. Wonfor, I feel like someone is screaming Timber, but the tree has not fallen yet.

He then replied, "Did you read the Wall Street Journal today?" I said," No, I haven't." He then replied, "You have got to be a Psychic. T. Boom Pickens wants to buy out Gulf and break it into many pieces." I said, "Wow." I left his office, and I started praying that would not happen. Not long after that, we were told that Gulf Oil sold the company to a small company whose headquarters was in California, Sun Oil, which later became Chevron USA. After that news, the CEO sent us all a letter.

At first, I was just going to throw it away, but I wanted to hear what the Head of Gulf Oil had to say. I opened the letter, read it and was about to throw the rest away. When something told me to keep these four and that someday they might be profitable. When I discovered that these were four shares given to me by my company, I thought maybe I would send them back to the CEO like the little boy in the bible with his five little loaves and two fish did. The CEO called me and personally said, "I thank you for sending me your shares, but I cannot accept them, and I will send them back to you." He also said, "I prayed about this move, and I know it is what the Lord wants me to do." I will explain in a future chapter what I did with my four little shares.

My boss had an assistant that I became very close to. I would tell her about Jesus, but she really did not want to hear that. Then, one day, she was promoted to our facility at the Drilling Technology Center. A couple of months later, I got a call from her telling me thank you for telling me about Jesus. I now have accepted Jesus Christ into my heart to stay.

Another lasting memory that I recall was when it was time to leave this home. My husband and I were thinking about trying to move next to his mom and dad so they would be able to take care of our daughter while we worked. One day, my husband and I were visiting his mom and dad, and they told us about a home that was under foreclosure next to his brother's. We went to check it out. We could only see the outside right then, but it was something we did like. I had already had a realtor looking, and she said the balance owed was still high.

She asked if we still wanted to look at it. I told her that I did not like to window shop and that if I could not buy it, I would not want to see it. She then said, "How much can you afford?" I told her a price that was nowhere close to what the bank was asking. At that moment, I found out my realtor was a Christian. She said, "Anything is possible if God is in it." So, she went to the bank on our behalf and told them what we could afford. She then came back and said that the bank said that we could go and look at it, and if we liked it, we could have it at the price we agreed.

My husband and I liked it very much, so we proceeded to apply for the loan. Then, one day, the loan officer called me and said they felt that we would be in financial trouble if we did not either lease or sell our previous home. They gave us very short notice, and if we were not able to do that, then our loan would not be approved. I remembered as though it were only yesterday. I had just got off the bus from work, and I was walking down the road, and my husband came to meet me. I told him that I heard from our loan officer, and I told him what they had said.

He said, "Hon, do not worry. We will pray about this." We prayed, "Father God, give us the time to make things right here. Help us to find what your will is here." Amen." The next day, I told my husband that I just wanted to go for a ride by myself and meditate on the Lord.

Leaving the house, a thought came to me. The thought was that when I returned, someone would come by who wanted to lease our house. When I returned, that is exactly what happened. A gentleman came and asked my husband about leasing our home there. Then, our realtor called and said that she also had someone. We chose the one that my husband met.

We were approved for the loan, and they told us that they would even pay our first month's light bill. I called that one of God's many favors.

But before we moved from my first home, there were some not so-good memories. I lost a brother, a sister, an aunt, a nephew, a grandmother, and two children, but still God was with me. He never left me, and He is never going to either. That is His promise to me.

SECOND HOME

In my second home, my immediate family began to grow rapidly. My son, Michael, got married, and his wife had a boy, Johnathan. They had a son together, Jeffrey.

Later years, he divorced her and married Spicelyn, whom he is still married to. They have two sons, Michael and Seth. Then there was my daughter, Kimberly, and she had David, Destiny, Daniel, and one who was adopted out, Brandon.

One thing I remember is when my son, Michael, came to me one night, and he said, "Mom, I did not want to tell you this; I quit school." I was in shock. I told him then what are you going to do? He told me that he was going to go to night school where his father was working and finish. The school told him he could still walk with his classmates on graduation. He did just that. I was proud of him.

Now, my daughter has a different story. She was becoming more difficult to handle. She got with the wrong crowd and started doing drugs. She had to be sent to an alternative school, and she was there in the ninth grade when she became pregnant. I decided to quit my job at Chevron to look after her.

When I retired from Chevron, I was to receive a large amount of money for 13 years of service. However, out of all the ones that retired, my paperwork got lost in the mail. I did not know what to do. I knew I had bills to pay. I did not want to lie and tell them that the check was in the mail. At that dire moment, I began to raise all my bills up toward Heaven, and I prayed, "Father God, you alone know my need; please help me here." As soon as I finished my prayer, my eyes turned to a scripture pertaining to Jubilee. A special year of remission of sins, debts, and universal pardon. I thought then of filing for bankruptcy.

So, we did. We still were able to keep our cars and home. It stayed on our credit for seven years, but God was with us, and we had all our needs met. I was reminded of the scripture in the bible, "Romans 8:28 "And we know that all things work together for the good of those who love God, to those who are called." The credit portion was poor but now it is excellent, thanks to my Almighty God.

Some not so-good memories there were when Billy lost his brother. His brother, John, lived next door, as I told you. Due to his battle with cancer, he became addicted to pain meds, lost his job and then lost his home, and moved in with us. He kept taking more medication to take care of his pain. One day, while I was working on an assignment, I called him, but I got no answer. When I returned home, his door was shut. I started to knock on his door, and something told me not to but to wait until Billy got home later that evening; I did just that. I went into the kitchen and saw that the breakfast I had prepared was not eaten. I felt something terrible had gone wrong. When Billy came in the door, I told him that he needed to go and check on his brother, and then I said without thinking, "He might be dead." I followed my husband to the room, and when he opened the door, I told him that he was gone. He was already blue and cold.

Then Billy also lost his dad while we were still living in our second home. His mom and dad were aging fast. His mom had been taking care of my daughter's child, Destiny. Destiny lived with them since she was a baby. She helped save their life one day.

They would always like to go to Greenpoint Mall to walk for exercise, but one day, they had to stay home because Destiny became ill. Thank God they did because that was the day when the Majic Johnson Theater's wall collapsed. Many people lost their lives that day, but Billy's mom and dad were spared because of my granddaughter, their great-granddaughter. Billy's mom was very attached to Destiny.

She would always tell me that if anyone took Destiny from her, she would just want to die. I told her not to think that way because God is the one who manners most, and He would see her through it when that happens. She never agreed. One day, not long after, my daughter's mother-in-law came and said she was taking Destiny to live with her. That very night, Billy's mom had a stroke and was taken by ambulance to the hospital.

Her stroke was bad, and she had to be placed in a nursing home. Billy's dad would visit her every day and stay till night. The home was cold, and his house was at a different temperature, so he came down with a bad cold. He was alone, so he came and stayed the night with us. He got sick, and we took him to the hospital.

He had pneumonia and then was placed in hospice at Kinder Care Hospital. One Sunday in Church, I had a strange feeling and told Billy he should go see his dad today because it could be the last time he would see him on this earth. We did, and the doctors told us that he caught a bad virus that did not respond to the antibiotics and that he was placed on a ventilator. Billy was able to talk to his dad about Jesus before, and he accepted Jesus into his heart that day before the ventilator was put in. He passed away the next day.

Another bad memory was when my sister-in-law, Alberta, passed away. She became ill, and her husband, Choice, and their granddaughter, Nora, came to live with us. Not long after, she was placed in hospice at home. One night, her husband and the nurse thought she was dying. They knocked on my door and said, "Come quickly; we think Alberta is dying. I went in there, and she was praying hard, and I asked her if she saw Jesus. She said, "No, I do not see Him." I then told her, "You are not leaving until you see Jesus." The following week, she was taken by ambulance to Ben Taub Hospital, and the doctors called Choice and me to come.

They said no medicine would help her now, so they took her off all the medicine. The family all came, and Pastor Steve Gatlin was there. I was sitting on my husband's lap because there were no more chairs. I looked over and saw that Alberta was saying something. I got off my husband's lap to go by her bedside to hear. I heard her say, "Jesus, I want to go home."

I told her to say it again, and this time, I would say it with her. I did, and immediately, the monitor displayed a flat line, and she was gone. I went back and sat on my husband's lap. When

I told the family what happened, they said they had never seen me get off Billy's lap. It was as if God slowed time for His glory.

THIRD HOME

Before this happened to his mom and dad, I was thinking of moving and buying a home together where my mother-in-law would have a larger kitchen, which she had always wanted.

Billy's dad would always tell me that all of us were too old to start over. I told him I did not think that way. After he passed, one night, I had a dream, and in the dream, Billy's dad came to me and said, "It is Ok for you to get a new home now." I thought that was strange, but I started looking. It took a good while because we saw many, but it just did not feel what God wanted for us. Our realtor at that time suggested building a new home in the Forest Ridge Subdivision. When we arrived there, I remembered being there when my daughter's mother-in-law, Annette, took us one time to show us the model of the home she bought. I had said then, "I would never live this far out, but my God had a different plan. Billy saw the home, and he fell in love with the model.

We would be closer to the church; North Central had moved from Aldine Westfield to its new location in Cypresswood.

One thing I remember very clearly is the first words my husband said to me when we entered our third home together.

He said, "This will be our little mansion down here until we get ours in Heaven." I said, "Amen." I never dreamed that would be a reality while we were living there. While we were waiting for our third home to be built, we attended a meeting where they discussed the layout of our home. They mentioned an extra bathroom would only be available If we signed our loan on a certain date. Otherwise, it would be an extra closet. I raised my hand and asked the lady what that date was. She told me, and I just turned to my husband and said, "The Lord gave us the extra bathroom by one day." If we had signed our loan papers one day after, we would have a closet instead of a guest bathroom. When we returned home, we both prayed and thanked God for His favor upon us.

I enjoyed many wonderful and blessed years there. Some of my best memories were there, and some of my worst were there, too. I learned to take the good with the bad, but always, the good outweighs the bad. As you recall, my mother-in-law was in the nursing home. Billy had retired, and he would visit her every day.

While visiting her, he started thinking of so many that could go out into eternity without God, and he asked the director if he could go into rooms and tell them about Jesus, and he told him he could. He did that, and at our church, there was a guy who did prison ministry, and he asked him if he could do it also. So, my husband did this ministry as well as the nursing homes until he became ill. Meanwhile, he was asked to provide services at two nursing homes in Houston, TX. One day after I retired in 2016, he asked me if I would join him and help him with the services at the nursing homes. I said, "I would." And I did for years until his illness became worse.

One day, while Billy was visiting his mom, the doctors told him that she had to be taken to the hospital because she was coughing and was having a hard time breathing. When she got to the hospital, they examined her, and she had pneumonia now in both lungs. They put her in the hospice, and not long after that, she passed away.

However, before she passed, I asked her if she saw Jesus, and she loudly said, "Yes." She did not speak to anyone but responded only when I asked her that. I remember telling her that she had one more job to do, and that would be when Destiny, her great-granddaughter, would be there to see her. I told her that I would ask her one more time if she could see Jesus. She did not respond. But when Destiny came in, I asked the question, and she immediately said, "Yes." However, that was the last time she spoke.

Another tragic event that happened was my loving husband of 48 years passed away while I lived there. Right after my husband passed away, Nora, Larry, and their two children came to live with me. Both my husband and I always thought of Nora as our very own child because she came to live with us when she was very young. I also refer to her two children as my grandchildren. This family became such a blessing and help. I was grieving over my husband's passing, and while they were there, I felt comfortable in my little mansion called home. They stayed with me for one year, and then they moved away.

After they moved, my little mansion contained too many memories, and it became bigger than I needed, so I decided to sell it and let someone else have it. I decided then to move in with my sister, Wanda. She always told me if I ever needed a home, her home would be it. My sister is turning 82, and I will be 75 this year. I asked her this one day, "Hey sister, have I changed from being a little monster to you when I was young?" She just laughed and said, "A little bit." Then she said, "Oh, I was just joking."

I do still drive her crazy in a good way, I believe. She must scream at me sometimes because I am deaf in one ear and can hardly hear out of the other, and she feels that when she does, other people think she is mad at me. We do help one another, and we are good company for each other. She is instrumental in recalling most of the events in my life; however, long ago, when I told her I was going to write this book. She said, "Just leave my chapter out." I told her then, "There was no way I could." I knew even back then that she would still play a major part in my life. I never imagined that I would ever move in with my sister until that horrible day came when I lost my loving husband.

THE DEATH OF MY HUSBAND

We bought our third home, which was our last in 2009. So, we still had twelve wonderful and blessed years together there. Billy became more ill in 2021. His blood pressure would become too low upon standing. He would have to lie down on the floor many times, and my daughter and I would try to pick him up. It was happening more frequently, and he finally said he did not want us to have to do that anymore.

So, he had me call an ambulance to take him to the hospital. In the hospital, they ran many tests, and finally, they decided to send him to a rehabilitation nursing home. There, they did not take care of him very well.

One day, I came just in time before he would fall out of a chair. They had him sit up in a chair to eat by himself. They took such poor care that he was found with horrible open bed sores, so bad they had to send him by ambulance to the hospital.

When the hospital examined him, they told me that he would need an operation because the open wound was bad. The next day, they checked his blood, and they said that his sodium level was too high, and they could not operate. Not long after that, they tested him for COVID, which was positive. The next day, his regular doctor came in to examine him.

Afterward, she called me and said, "There is no medicine I can give him that will help. All I suggest is that you plan to make him as comfortable as possible."

At that moment, I just froze. My heart felt like it was coming out of my chest. I knew what she meant. My loving husband would now be placed in Hospice. At the time, I was unable to visit him because I had caught the virus myself and I was very ill. I thought I was dying. The male nurse who oversaw taking care of my husband asked me if I wanted him to come home. I did not want to see him like that. I wanted to remember him as being energetic and healthy. But God had His plan.

The next day, the nurse asked if he could just bring him home because of the insurance. He said that when he transitioned, he would pick him back up. I reluctantly said yes, and to this day, I am very glad I did. I made room for the cot in the living room. The hospital brought him in on a Saturday. I remember they had balloons tied to the stretcher because the hospital celebrated his birthday while he was in the hospital.

His birthday was October 4, 1947. They were bringing him home on October 9, 2021. When he was brought in, I saw that he had lost so much weight that I became sick to my stomach. His body was already decomposing. They had stopped feeding him. He had oxygen. He never opened his eyes, and he never spoke a word. My daughter, Kimberly, as I told you before, took very good care of him. She turned on his favorite Christian music and his favorite Western shows. She sat at his bedside all night. During the night, I prayed, "Father God, please let my husband pass away at home where his family is." Then I heard a voice say, "Child, I could not speak to you until now because you would not have been able to bear it. But I have prepared you for this hour, and now you will venture into a new chapter in your life."

The next morning was Sunday. I will never forget it as long as I live. My daughter had our church, North Central, on. I went into the room and sat beside him. Michael, his son, called him on the phone and told him that he loved him and that he should just rest. After that, I prayed for him and spoke in tongues. Then I saw a big smile on his face, and he went out peacefully. On October 10, 2021, my handsome, loving, devoted Christian husband got his mansion up there.

I had his funeral at the graveside, and it was beautiful. The following are the words I penned:

We are gathered here today at this gravesite to say our goodbyes to Billy Joe Cross, date of birth October 04, 1947 – date of homecoming October 10, 2021.

But as for me, I won't say goodbye, but I will say it until we meet again. For in John 3:16, it says, For God so loved the world that He gave his only begotten son and whoever believes in Him shall not perish; but have eternal life. Billy and I both believed this with all our hearts.

Now, Billy Cross wears many hats in this world. The most important one was he was a devout servant of the Lord. As many of you may know, he went to prison to share the gospel. He also shared the word in many nursing homes.

He would witness to every person he met. He wanted everyone to find Jesus like he did. He never compromised his belief, and he never strayed. He stayed on the straight and narrow path, just like the word of God said.

Billy also wore the hat as a father. He was called Daddy to you, and he loved you greatly. He would pray for you every night, and his greatest desire was for you to be saved.

He wore the hat of Papaw. He loved you with all his heart. He would pray for you every night, and his greatest desire was for you to be saved.

Lastly but in my eyes, what was first to me. He was a faithful, dedicated husband of mine for 48 years. He was kind and thoughtful, and he always prayed for me.

Now, I would like for us to bow our heads and pray, Father, we thank you for allowing us to know and love your servant, Billy Cross, my loving husband, our dad, and our grandfather for all these short years. Father, God help us strive to follow his example. We know that each of us here is given a certain time here on this earth. So, Father, I pray that by the grace and mercy of God, we can say, not our goodbyes today; we can all say until we meet again. In Jesus' name, we prayed, and everyone said Amen.

A year after my husband passed, I began to realize that my home had become too big and too lonely. I decided to move in with my sister, Wanda; I am still with her today.

RETURNING TO MY HOME CHURCH

Before I tell you the story about how I decided to return to my home church, I need to give you some background. As you recall, my family was attending the Bethel Pentecostal Church of God. I was a member there when I was three years old. My family and I attended there for over 35 years. We were, as I discussed earlier, the custodians of the church, and I was one of the Sunday School Teachers. I had many wonderful memories there. Of course, I was married there.

Both my children were born while I was still attending Bethel Church. One memory I recall was having a record made by Bethel's pianist and dear friend, Lisa Martinez. Do you remember the four Gulf Oil shares I told you about in the previous chapters? One day, I was running to catch my bus for work, and I almost missed it. I got on and began to say from within, "Thank you, Lord, I made it to the bus in time." I remembered, and then a song came to me. In fact, two songs came to my mind. When I reached work, I wrote them down. The titles were "I am The God That Heals Thee and Take These Burdens from My Heart and Set Me Free." After writing them down, I felt the Spirit telling me that they were not given just for me but for anyone who wanted to listen. I figured I would have them put on a record. A miracle happened, and I found out about a recording studio nearby and asked about the price. The price was the exact amount of money I received from selling my four shares of stock from Gulf Oil. The songs were recorded by Lisa Martinez on a record, and many records were made.

One day, a visiting evangelist from Mexico came and ministered at Bethel, and I donated the records to him to help build a church in Mexico. Another memory of mine there at Bethel was when I observed Lisa's young son, Ricky. He was such a handsome boy and very compassionate to others. I can recall him walking down the church aisle carrying a bucket and collecting change for the church. All the young children would be signing "Building Up the Temple for The Lord." That was one event in our church that I really looked forward to, seeing all those small children serving the Lord.

I left Bethel and joined North Central, and I will explain more about that. However, my sister, Wanda, had told me that little Ricky, who was then a youth pastor at Bethel, was going to preach the next night. I told her I wanted to be there, and I did come. After the preaching, I shook his hand and said, "I sure enjoyed your preaching, and you are going to be a fine preacher someday." He replied, "No, mam, I am going to be a lawyer." I then replied, "Well, if that is what you think."

He became that preacher at Bethel, and I will discuss that in more detail later in this chapter.

Now that I have given you some background, I will tell you what happened and why I left Bethel. If you recall, after Pastor A. L. Gatlin passed away, the church voted in Pastor Gary Cox, and after Pastor Cox resigned, Pastor Wilburn was voted in. I had heard that Brother Cox was going to be preaching at a church in Houston at Trinty on a Sunday night. Billy and I never missed a service except this time. A strange thing happened. I was standing up and singing with the rest of the congregation when suddenly, a voice within me said, "What would you do if I took you from your church?" From within, I replied, "No, I do not want to leave my church." My thought was that we were the custodians of the church, not that I was a Sunday School teacher.

The next weekend, we did not get to clean the church because our son, Michael, became very ill. That Sunday morning, Pastor Wilburn asked why the church did not get cleaned, and we told him that Michael had gotten sick at the last moment and that we were unable to come. He became upset, and words were spoken that I had taken out of context. At the time, I did not realize that he was expecting family and a new group to come that Sunday. However, I was upset, and I told Billy that I would not be coming back. That night, everyone asked where I was, and Billy told them that I would not be coming back.

That night, I cried out to the Lord, "Father God, why did you take me from my church where all my friends were?" The voice within said, "If I hadn't said so, it would not have been my will. I have other friends I want you to meet."

The next day, Billy asked me to go to North Central church with him because they were having a revival. I did not want to go because I just did not feel like meeting any new people. Billy insisted that he was going, and the moment he was out of sight, all the lights in the neighborhood went out. I questioned the Lord and asked, "Should I have gone back to Bethel?" The voice within said, "No, but when your husband returns, he will say," "I do not know about you, but I have found my church." Guess what happened when he returned?

The moment he walked in the door, all the lights came back on, and he said, "I do not know about you, but I have found my church." I just laughed out loud. He said, "I do not see anything funny in that." Then I told him what happened, and he then said, "It must be a sign from the Lord." The next service night, I was there, and it felt so much like home. They were singing some of the same songs that we sang at Bethel. I had some good times there and met some nice people, just like the Lord said I would. My daughter and my grandchildren were all baptized there. My daughter was only seven years old when we first came to North Central. My son, Michael, was fourteen at the time.

I was a Sunday School teacher and watched many of my students grow up to be adults working in the church, some with the Children's ministry. One time, I was in the nursery with my grandson, and a lady came with a baby. She told me that her husband and her had adopted his sister's baby. She had been told by her doctors that she would not be able to carry a child full term.

However, she wanted to have one of her very own. I told her that I would be praying for her. One evening, not long after that, the alter call was given, and she went up for prayer. I stood in front of her and prayed, "Father, God, your faithful servant stands before you in faith that you answer her prayer."

Seven months went by, and one Sunday night, my husband came in from church, and he said that Mary's husband had said thank you because they were having a child of their own. She not only had one, but a year later, she had another one.

At North Central, I got to know a lot of wonderful people. My Sunday School teachers, brother and sister Wilson, were always very nice to me and always ready to hear whatever I had to say. Other dear friends that I remember were brother and sister Wells. I knew Brother Wells because he was my biology and Algebra teacher in high school. I remember raising my hand and asking him if he believed in evolution. He told me that he would speak to me in private after class. When the bell rang, he called me and said, "I do not believe in evolution, but I must teach it.

Another memory of Brother Wells is what he said when I was in his Algebra Class. He said, "Emily, that is the name I ask to be called because I thought the name Emma was too old-fashioned." He would still call me Emily, even in Sunday School.

In Algebra class, after class, he stopped me and said, "Emily, you were my A+ student in biology, and you are a C in Algebra." I just smiled and said, "Math is not my bag." I cannot believe I said that to my teacher. I enjoyed seeing and knowing him in Sunday School class all over again. I felt very blessed to know that he was a Christian even back then. Sadly, he passed away while I was still attending North Central.

His wife came also and her testimony, I will never forget. She told me that years back she went into the hospital to have heart surgery. That night before surgery, a nurse came in and explained everything to her and told her not to be afraid that she would be fine. She left, leaving her name with her. The next morning, when the nurses came in to get her ready for surgery, she told them about the nurse who had come to her last night and told her everything. The nurses then said to her, "Sorry, but we do not have a nurse that works here by that name." Sister Wells then realized she had been visited by an angel that night.

Pastor Emerson was a great pastor, very kind and compassionate with me. He even paid our light bill one time when we were unable to pay it. When the church moved, he resigned, and his son, Pastor Larry Emerson, took over. He was just like his dad, a very good preacher and pastor as well. Over the years, I heard some wonderful sermons from both.

My family and I continued attending North Central for over 30 years until I heard from the Lord once more. This time I was talking to pastor Larry Emerson about Billy's memorial service. As we began discussing how my husband and I first met, a voice within said, "It is time to go back home to Bethel."

At first, I just shoved it off, but when another sad event happened, I realized the time was now. As I recall, I told you that when Pastor Steve Gatlin retired from Bethel, Pastor Rick Martinez was voted in. Pastor Steve Gatlin and his wife started attending North Central after that because his son and daughter-in-law were attending there. Many years passed by, and in the year of 2022, Pastor Steve Gatlin passed away. Pastor Rick Martinez was one of the ones who officiated part of Pastor Steve Gatlin's service. It was held at North Central Church. After the service was over, I spoke to Pastor Rick, and that is when, without thinking, I said, "I am returning home." He did not say a word, and I know why. He knew it was wrong to influence anyone to change the church that they attend faithfully. So, I did hear the voice of God, and this time, he told me to go back home to Bethel. I did, and I know I have been greatly blessed because I know without a doubt that I am in God's will. I am looking forward to many more blessed years at home in Bethel.

If you recall, in previous chapters, I told you that the Lord told me that I would write a book. I wrote not only one book but five others, and this one makes up six. They can all be found on Amazon and various other stores. The titles are: "A Nightmare in Hell," "Welcome to My Garden," Part I, "Welcome To My Garden Part II, Welcome To My Garden Part III, "Spirit Power," and then this one you are reading now, "A Life More Abundantly." I can say faithfully that it would not have been possible if it hadn't been for the help of the good Lord above and for my publishers.

Now, I would like to turn your attention to something new and inspiring. I would like to title it "Word from The Lord."

WORDS FROM GOD

And. over the years, ever since I accepted Jesus Christ into my heart, the Lord has given me His own little book of words. His book of words consists of letters to certain people, even past Presidents of the United States of America, visions, dreams, and even songs. I hope that you will enjoy reading each one. The first words will have no date on them. The others will have a date when the Lord gave them to me.

WITH JESUS AT GALILEE

The other night I was praying to the Lord. Now I do not recall if I had a dream or a vision; but suddenly, I was in the very presence of Jesus Christ at the Sea of Galilee.

Jesus asked me if I saw the big boat out there in the sea and I said Yes, Lord, I do. He then began telling me of the time His disciples had fished all night but caught nothing. He then said when he told them to cast their nets on the other side and they obeyed; their catch was very great, and it broke the nets. He asked me if I remembered the story and I said, yes, Lord I do. Then He asks me this question,

"Do you know that a lot of my disciples were fishermen by trade? I replied, yes Lord, I do. Then Jesus said to me, "Child I am a carpenter, and I make things." I made you, my child."

I said, I know my Lord and I am so grateful you did."

He then placed His hand on my shoulder and said, "My child, I made you for a purpose and I have great plans for you; plans not to harm you; but plans to prosper you and be in good health as your soul prospers. My desire for you is to do great and mighty things through me if you will and I answered, I will. I said it the second time, I will, and as I said it the third time,

I heard the voice of my Pastor, Larry Emerson, repeat the words, I will and when he said it the third time.

I heard our church shout out three times, "I will, I will, I will.

And at that moment, my dream or vision ended, and I found myself in awe of what had just happened to me. I prayed to Jesus and thanked Him for allowing me to have such a beautiful dream or vision. I thanked Him for allowing the words of my Pastor to be deeply rooted in my heart and mind. Then I said that if You, Jesus, would, I will, by the grace of almighty God; do great and mighty works through you, my Lord Jesus, who strengthens me.

A VISIT FROM JESUS

My story begins in this way. Last night, Friday, November 30, 2019, I laid my head down to sleep and suddenly I became sick to my stomach. I began praying over and over "Jesus, please let this pass and after a while, I began to feel well again. I was so thankful, and I just started repeating over and over to Jesus, "Thank you, Jesus, for all you have done for me. I said, "Thank you, Jesus, for saving me, forgiving me, and most of all for loving me and making a way for me to be with you in Heaven someday. Then I heard the voice of Jesus say to me, "Child, I would like to talk with you." I replied," l am ready now to hear."

Jesus then said this to me, "He said, Child, I take all your plans and make them mine." I said, "My Lord, do you not mean it to be the other way around." He said, "No child, come I will show you."

At that moment, I felt his arms around me and in my spirit, I knew where He was going to take me, and I did not want to go there so he had to gently push me along the way. I kept telling Him that I did not want to see Him on the Cross. I did not want to see again all the suffering and pain that He went through. He said, "My child, without the cross, all would be lost. Everyone wants to see the beauty, but no one wants to see the ashes. Child, I bring beauty out of ashes.

Then He ask me this question, "Do you remember what the thief on my left said to me? l said, Yes, l do." He said, "So you are the Messiah, are you? Prove it by saving yourself and us, too." Jesus said, "You are right and what did the one on the right say? I said, He said, "Don't you even fear God when you dying? We deserve to die for our evil deeds, but this man hasn't done one thing wrong." Then he said, "Jesus, remember me when you come into your Kingdom." This is right also, child and what did I say back to him? Jesus, you said, "Today you will be with me in Paradise. That is right. So now can you understand that I take all your plans and make them mine? I said, I believe I do. It is just like the scripture says, "We know that all things work together for good to those who love God, to those who are called according to His purpose." Jesus then said, my child you are right again; but it is not for you only but for all those you do acknowledge me as their Messiah. I will always take their plans and make them mine. I will always bring beauty out of ashes, and I will always cause all things, good and bad to work together for the good for those who love me, to those who are called according to my purpose which is their

Eternal home with me forever and forever.

After this, I came to my computer to type this all down so I would not forget my visit with Jesus. I also went to the internet and found some inspiring messages regarding my visit with Jesus' tonight. I do not understand why this all happen to me this night; but I do know from experience that when the visitations come; He always has a plan to give me guidance and heads up regarding anything.

I had said my prayers for the night and then I heard this voice within say, "Child I would like to talk with you." I recognized Jesus's voice to me, and I answered immediately, "Sure I would love to talk with you. Let's have a fireside chat. We have not had one in a while now."

Jesus said, Sure we can do that. Let's gather the wood for the fire and we did it together. The fire was made, and we sat down across from each other. Jesus then asks me what story from the Bible, I want Him to talk about. I said, since It was going to be Mother's Day tomorrow, let me hear the one where you did something special for your mother, Mary." He replied. Ok, but I would like to hear the story from you." I said, oh, you are trying to see I know my Bible. Is that right?" Jesus said, yes, my child. Now go on and tell me the story."

I said, " I believe It happened in a town called, Cana. There was a wedding feast and your mother, Mary, and you and your disciples were there. Jesus said, Yes, child go on." I said,

The next day there was a wedding celebration in the village of Cana in Galilee. Jesus' mother was there, and Jesus and his disciples were also invited to the celebration. The wine supply ran out during the festivities, so Jesus' mother told him, they have no more wine.

"Dear woman, that's not our problem," Jesus replied. My time has not yet come."

After that l asked Jesus this question, why did your mother, Mary know that you would be able to meet her need when it was not yet your time? Jesus answered and said to me, Child, my mother already knew that l was the Son of the Living God, and that l loved her very much and would do anything to meet her need at the time even if it was not yet my time. And my child, l will do the same for you because you know that I am the Son of the Living God, and that l love you very much and it is my pleasure to do for you whatever you ask; but you must trust and keep the faith." I then said, Jesus, can l ask you another question? Promise you won't get mad at me. l do not mean to be ugly about It." Jesus said, my child, I already know how you feel so Just ask me anything." I said, Jesus, l have been praying about my needs but l have not seen a confirmation that they will be met." Jesus said, My

Child, do you not know that I have told you that you must trust me and keep the faith." At that moment, Jesus said, now go on with the rest of the story." I said Ok, but his mother told the servants, do whatever he tells you.

"Standing nearby were six stone water Jars, used for Jewish ceremonial washing. Each could hold twenty to thirty gallons."! Jesus told the servant, Fill the jars with water." When the jars had been filled, he said, now dip some out, and take it to the master of ceremonies." So, the servants followed his instructions.

"When the master of ceremonies tasted the water that was now wine, not knowing where It had come from (though, of course, the servants knew), he called the bridegroom over.

And said, The host always serves the best wine first, then, when everyone has had a lot to drink, he brings out the less expensive wine. But you have kept the best until now!"

Jesus then said, "Child go and tell my children that if they know that I am the Son of the Living God and that I love them and if they keep trusting and holding on to their faith In Me that I will always meet their needs according to my riches in Glory."

LAST NIGHT IN GALILEE

Last night, I seemed to be hurting all over; so, I asked Jesus to take me to Galilee. Jesus replied, "Just because I take you to galilee, doesn't mean all your pains will go away." I said, "Just take me anyway." while there in Galilee, I told Jesus that I wanted to do his will and be what he wanted me to be. I asked him what he wanted me to do. Jesus said, "Child, just keep doing what you have been doing." keep encouraging and helping others. Keep sharing the gospel and leading souls to my kingdom. I said, "I will" then Jesus said, "Are you ready to go back now?" I said, "No, I want to stay with you forever." Jesus then said, "Do you want to go to heaven?"

I thought, would I be able to get in? Have I done enough for Jesus to get into heaven? Jesus and I were standing at the beautiful gate and Jesus just looked at me and I thought this is it. I am not going to be able to go in. Thank God, I was wrong. Jesus just said to the man over the gate, "She is with me and then the gates open wide, and we went inside. It was very beautiful. Just like the bible says, human words cannot express what joys awaits a child of God when he or she gets to heaven.

I saw some of my relatives and one asked me this question, 'you here now?" l said, "No, I am just visiting. I am coming back though, when we partake of the lord's supper of the lamb together."

Written: 03/02/2024

Last night while I was praying; I ask Jesus if he was here with me. He replied yes, my child I am here". Then I asked him if he would stay with me all night and he said, "Yes, my child I will.

Soon after that he began speaking to me and it was in such a stern voice that I had not heard before. He said, "My child I am not pleased with this world. Evil is ever present in their minds. They have become proud and haughty. They do not

Obey me and my commandments, they do ungodly wrongs in my sight. I have given them space after space to repent; but they have not. Instead, they have hardened their hearts against me and no longer fear me. I have turned them over to a redebate mind and judgment will soon follow. Soon they will feel my wrath upon them and then they will know that I am the great I am, the Alpha and the Omega, the beginning and the end, thus said the Lord".

April 21, 2019

Last night I had a dream. I dreamed I was sitting on top of a huge rock by the shores of Galilee. As Always it was my place of peace. I could feel the soft breeze on my back. I could smell the fresh air from the sea, and I could hear the waves.

Then suddenly, I noticed I did not see Jesus. I always saw him when I went there in my visions or dreams, but this time seemed different. I hollered out His Name, "Jesus where are you? I heard His voice say, Child I am right here.: I replied where, I cannot see you." Jesus asks me to close my eyes, and I obeyed. Immediately then I saw Him. I said, "Thank God, I can see you now." Jesus then said, "Child do not see things as the world sees them. I created you in the likeness and image of me and down deep inside of you is my spirit and whenever you want to see me; just look for me within your beautiful spirit and I will always be there. You know I said I would never leave you nor forsake you here." I said, yes, Jesus I do know that is true.

Now, I want to ask you this question: "With all the evil in the world today; do you still have peace?"

I answered yes because I know I will always have you.

Jesus answered very good." You know I created you to not understand all things; but to trust and love me with all your heart, mind, soul and strength. I want you to know that everything in this world is going exactly as I planned.

Jesus then said, "Child, will you do something for me?" I said, sure lord, I will do anything for you."

Go back and tell my people not to give up on me

Now. Even though this world is in a very broken place with evil all around. Tell them to

Keep trusting and loving me with all their hearts, minds, souls, and strength. Tell them that soon and very soon, I will be coming for them. The dead in Christ will rise first and those that are alive and remain will be changed like a twinkling of an eye and will be caught up together to meet me in the air. I will then take them to the place I have prepared for them in heaven where I will be with them forever and ever.

This was written on 09/04/2017, 3:00 a.m. In the morning

Last night I was praying for all my grandchildren and your face came before me. I heard the voice of the lord say, "My child, you know me when you need me and when you no longer need me.

You hardly know me. The Holy Spirit went on to say, "There is a way that seems right to a man, but its end is the way of

death. Call on me now while I am near. Let the wicked change their ways and banish the very thought of doing wrong.

Let them turn to the lord that he may have mercy on them. Yes, turn unto me; for I will forgive you generously."

Study my word. It is a lamp for your feet to see the right way to go.

"My word will teach you to trust in me at all times. It will disciple you to trust and love me with all your heart. For my child, you must love me with all your heart, all your soul, all your mind, and all your strength. The second is equally important for my child: love your neighbor as much as yourself. Who is your neighbor, my child, anyone that needs me."

"After I heard these sayings, the holy spirit then said this to me, "What I have just told you, concerning your grandchildren; is not for them only; but for all those who have need of me."

Then I knew that the lord wanted me to post this for all to see and for them to pass it on. John 3:16 says, "For God so loved the world, that he gave his only Son, so that everyone who believes in him may not perish but have eternal life."

Written: 12/30/2014, 2:00 PM.

Last night, I asked Jesus if we could go to Galilee because I wanted to just bow at his feet and thank him for everything, almost in an instant when we were there.

Tears were falling ferociously from my eyes, and I told Jesus that I wanted to wash his feet with my tears and dry them with my hair like Mary did in the bible. I forgot though my hair is short now. I said Jesus my spirit is willing. Jesus then asked me, "Child what is it that you want to thank me for? I said, my Lord, I want to thank you for everything. I want to thank you for coming into this world to save me. I want to thank you for forgiving me, loving me, and setting me free. I want to thank you for making a way for me to spend eternity with you. I want to thank you for what Isaiah said, you were wounded for my transgressions, you were bruised for my annuities, the chastisement of your peace is up on me and by your stripes I am healed I know you have come now, and I thank you. I thank you for shedding your blood for me on Calvary. You have purchased me with your blood. I have been blood-bought and blood-redeemed. Thank you, thank you.

Then Jesus said, all these I have done for you; but they are not for you only but for all those who come to me and seek me with all their heart, strength, mind and soul. I came and died for every person in this world, and I came to do unto them that which I have done unto you. Then Jesus paused and asked this question, "Child why have not the thousands upon thousands and more not come to thank me as you have this day?"

Then Jesus answered his own question in this manner. He said, "Let this not worry you, my child, for the scriptures say that one day every knee will bow, and every tongue will confess that I am Jesus Christ, the Lord.

Believe It or Not

A Warning From God

What I am about to say is of the truth and nothing but the truth so help me God.

You could say I am psychic. If I lived in the days of Joan of Arc; I would have been burned alongside of her because of her claims she heard from God.

What I am about to tell you will be a shock to some and a warning for others.

It begins during the times of former President Clinton and the former President bush were in the White House I wrote them both concerning my concerns. However, they never listened.

What is concerning me now is the series of events that have happened since 2008. The night John McCain and Obama were in debates, I was woken up by the Holy Spirit at 3:00 am. In the morning and the voice said, "Yee shall have a black president, but the church will be going."

From that time on, I started checking on the internet and watching for signs of the end. I discovered that many people have dreams of large earthquakes and tsunamis coming on the earth. There were other predictions as well, at least enough to merit that something big was happening to our world.

From 2008 until now, I have been watching the world news as it unfolds the present world situation. During President Obama's second term during their convention, they said they wanted to leave God out I begin praying, "Lord, let there be a David in the house. That is when the Holy Spirit gave me the poem, "Let There Be a David in the House which you can find in one of my books.

During his formal address to the nation, from within myself, I suddenly spoke one word, when. The Holy Spirit began speaking to me and said, "The eyes of March." The only thing I remember about that was when Brutus murdered Julius Ceasar. Then I heard on the news that March is when all the revolution started in the Middle East.

Then this Sunday, March 26, 2010, before Sunday service, I ask from within, "Lord what are you trying to tell your people today?" The Holy Spirit brought to my remembrance Psalms 111. "The fear of the Lord is the beginning of all wisdom." Then the words came, tell my people that I love then and that I see their faults and look beyond them, and I can see their needs. I met them all when I went to the cross, died and rose again. Tell them to repent and re dedicate themselves to me.

Written: 3/15/2014, 2:30 AM

I asked the Holy Spirit to take me to Galilee and there I was.

Once again, I express how much I enjoyed being there once more in the presence of my Lord.

I enjoyed walking barefoot in the warm sands and feeling the warm breeze coming off the ocean.

After a time, Jesus said, "Child what would you like to do while you are here with me this time?"

I replied, "I would like to have a fireside chat with you."

Jesus said OK and He built a fire, and we sit down and then He said, "What would you like to talk about today."

I said, "Jesus I want to be ready when you come back for your church."

Child, He replied, "You are ready. You are eagerly looking forward to my coming and you try as best as you can with the help of the Holy Spirit to do that which is right in my sight.

Then I said, I feel sorry for all the others that you died for, and they do not understand the urgency of the hour. And then I said, Jesus what in the world are they thinking?"

Child, He said, 'What they are thinking is they have plenty of time to get things right." They do not realize that I can change things in a twinkling of an eye and then it would be too late."

All they need to do is repent, come unto me, leave their sins behind them, and follow me.

Because strait is the gate, and narrow is the way, which led unto life, and few there be that find it.

A LETTER TO GOD

Written: 09/03/2013

Dear God,

I am writing to tell you how much I love you and to ask you what you would want me to do for you.

You already know how much I love you because you have looked upon my heart. I know indeed that we are living in the very last days before your son, Jesus Christ will come and take his waiting bride. I believe we are just waiting for you to say the word.

Meanwhile, will you please speak to me and let me know how I can fit into the completion of your plan for mankind?

Child, listen very carefully to what I am about to say to you. Many people claim to know the right thing to do yet they do not. They say they belong to me; yet they do not.

On that day I will say to them go away I never knew you. They claim that they were led by me and that they were a slave to me, yet that is not the truth. They were not led by me at all; but by the devil and have become his slave. They conform to the world and their fleshly desires and not to me and my godly desires.

Some sat in the pews every church service, yet they do not serve me or know me. There are those in high places who claim what they do is for the good of all mankind, yet they are greatly deceived. The very things that they say are good for mankind will bring utter destruction in the end for I will come like a thief in the night and destroy that which remains.

The only good for mankind, my child, is to acknowledge they have a savior in my son, Jesus Christ who shed his blood for them all and to repent of their evil deeds and take up their cross and follow him. Then I will be their God, and they will be my people. Behold, I want you to speak these words in season or not, 2"Timothy 4 "I charge thee therefore before God, and the lord Jesus Christ, who shall judge the quick and the dead at his appearing and his kingdom; 2" preach the word; be instant in season, out of season; reprove, rebuke, exhort with all longsuffering and doctrine. 3" for there will come a time when they will not endure sound doctrine; but after their lusts shall they heap to themselves teachers, having itching ears; 4" and they shall turn away their ears from the truth and shall be turned unto fables. 5th but you watch therefore and, in all things, endure afflictions, do the work of an evangelist, and make full proof of the ministry."

Written: 11/01/ 2012

Last night I had a dream and in that dream; I was at a doctor's office. I was there for some government reason. I do not know what. The doctor said he was going to give me a shot for Diabetes. He said it might kill me. I said, "Oh no, I do not want to die. At that moment, I woke up from my dream and my head was hurting. I took a Tylenol and lad back down. I heard a still small voice say, "Let me take you to Galilee.' I said, "Might as well; I have a headache anyway.

Jesus said to me, "I know all your concerns and I will address them in a little while. Then He said, "Child, it has been a while since we had a fire side chat. You go and take a nice swim, and I will prepare the wood and fire for our chat." When I came from my swim, I was very cold and shaking. Jesus very gently placed a blanket around me, and I sat down by the cozy fire. Jesus then began speaking to me.

He said, child, "I know you want your daughter, my child, delivered and your son also my child. At that moment, I interrupted Jesus and said, "Your child, he does not even have his eyes open toward you. That may be but he is still my child. They are all my children. I quickly apologized and Jesus told me to keep on praying and believing. Do not look at the circumstances but look unto Him, "the author and finisher of my faith.

Then Jesus said, Child, I know you questioned whether you will be ready when I come because of your feeling that everything was looking better for you in the world right now. Then Jesus asked me this question, "Child, how do you feel right now?' I said, "I feel great, nice and warm and cozy here with you.' He then said, "Child, are you ready to go back now?' I said no, 'I love being here with you.' Jesus then said these words to me, "Child there will always be a fire in your heart, mind and soul as long as you keep them stayed upon me."

Written: 4/16/2012

Last night, in a vision, Jesus asked me to go to Galilee with Him. I said, "Yes." Suddenly we were there. Jesus looked up at me and said, "Would you like to take a walk with me, child?" I said, "Yes I would love to walk alongside of you." We hadn't walked very far when suddenly; Jesus stopped and turned to me and asked me this question. "" Child what do you see?" I replied, "I can see the beautiful sea of Galilee and the beautiful sands on which we are standing on now." Jesus replied, "But what else can you see?" "That is all I can see." "Child, close your eyes and I immediately obeyed. Then He said, "Child, open your eyes and I obeyed. Then he asked me this question, what can you see now?" I said with much excitement in my voice, "O my God, I see angels all around me." Jesus replied, "Indeed they are. I have given my angels charge over you to protect you, not only you but for every child of God."

Written: 07/14/2020

Today, would like to share with all of you something very unusual that happened to me, but before I begin, I need to give you some background on what happened first.

On Monday night, July 13th, 2020, I was meditating with the Lord and I begged Him to speak to me because I had not heard from Him in a while; but nothing came. So, then I begged Him to speak to me in a dream. I thought He would, but He did not.

Later that evening, on July 14, 2020, I was watching the World News on TV and as soon as I turned off the TV; the Holy Spirit got a hold of me right there alone by the kitchen table and I begin to speak in other tongues. I spoke for about three minutes and then something that had never happened to me before occurred. I began singing in tongues. It sounded so pretty. I knew it could not have come from me.

Afterwards, I believe the Holy Spirit gave me the interpretation.

The following is that interpretation:

"It is I the Lord your God. Do not be afraid. I have not given you the spirit of fear but of love and a sound mind. I promised you that I would never leave nor forsake you. Know that I am here even with you now. I am God, the Alpha and Omega the beginning and the end. I am the everlasting One. I your God will allow what I will, and I will stop what I want to stop. I will show the whole world that I am God, all powerful and mighty in their site. I will show them signs both in the air and on the earth that I am God, and I am coming for my own soon. Those that repent and accept me as their Lord and Savior; I will take with me and those who do not will stay to suffer the horrible things that will be coming upon this earth. I want you to know this, my child, that I am in full control. Do not look to the left nor to the right; but look unto me, the author and finisher of your faith. Many will come to try to destroy your faith, but I say unto you, hold on, hold on to your faith for that same faith will bring you home. Always remember this, I am and forever will be in full control."

After that, I told the Lord thank you giving this to me and I heard a voice within say, "You are welcome, now child tell the world thus saith the Lord."

Written: 04/11/2020

It was 1:31 a.m. on a Saturday morning when I had this dream that I was talking to Jesus. I asked him if he could reveal to me the things to come just as he did to John the revelator in the book of Revelations. I told him that I wanted to be the voice of truth and not half-truth but the truth and this is what I heard him say, "My child, I have heard the cries and prayers of my people, and I will heal their lands for a short period of time. In this short period of time, I will draw them to me. For no one can come unto the father unless he be drawn and I want to do this more than ever because I am coming soon and I wish that no man perishes, but that all would be saved. In this short period of time, I will perform many miracles through my children. My children will be my voice, and I will tell them the words to say, and many souls will be saved in those days and my children will be liken unto the church of Philadelphia"

Then Jesus repeated the words of Revelations 3:8-11

"I have placed before you an open door that no man can shut. I know you have little strength, yet you have kept you have kept my word and have not denied my name. I will make those who are of the synagogue of Satan, who claim to be Jews though they are not, but are liars I will make them come and fall at your feet and acknowledge that I have loved you. Since you have kept my command to endure patiently, I will also keep you from the hour of trial that is going to come upon the whole world to test those who live on the earth. I am coming soon. Hold on to what you have, so that no one take your crown."

Written: 09/16/2009

Last night I had a beautiful talk with my Lord. After saying my nightly prayer, I started repeating His name repeatedly. Then Jeus ask me this question. "Why do you like calling out my name repeatedly?" I answered him in this manner. I said, "Because your name is beautiful. There is no other name by which man can be saved." I went on to say, "Your name is power. Your name is Healing. You said to pray in your name and believe what I pray for and then I shall have it. Most of all your name is love." After I said that, Jesus looked at me and asked this question. "Child, what do you mean by love?" I said, "In your Name there is complete love. You loved me enough to sacrifice your life's blood by hanging on an old, rugged cross for me." Jesus looked at me with such compassion in his eyes and said, "Yes, child, and I would gladly do it again if I had too. That is how much I love you, but not only is you that same love for all my children, your children and your children's also." I then said, "Even my littlest one?" He replied, even for him." At that moment, I started crying out with joy. Then I asked him if he could find favor in his eyes for me like he did for Noah? I said, "Jesus you helped Noah build a huge boat "He replied, "Yes I did and your children and children's childrens will be saved because I obeyed my father and gave my blood to save them all and I will prepare their hearts to follow me."

Written: 10/20/2006

I had an encounter with Jesus last night. I asked Him to order my steps. I told him I wanted to be completely led by Him.

He asked me this question, "Do you know what this means?"

He went on to say, this means you want to be a righteous person. For it says in my word, the steps of a righteous man are ordered by the Lord.

I answered, "Yes, Lord. Help me to be righteous.

Then suddenly I was in a vision where Jesus took me to Galilee, my favorite place by the sea. Jesus asked me to follow him. I said, "Yes I will obey."

Jesus started walking a few steps away from me. He was taking very small steps. Then he turned and asked me, "Child, can you follow me?"

I said, "Sure, why are you taking such small steps?" Jesus answered and said, "My child, if I took larger steps away from you; you would not be able to follow me.

Jesus then asks me, that is what you want to do right? You want to follow and have your steps ordered by me?"

I answered quickly, "Yes, Lord let us begin."

Jesus then said to me, "Child you can be anywhere in the world and still feel my presence with you. You can be at work, in your car, on the streets of the city. You see child, you hear by voice, and it makes me rejoice. I know you. I know my sheep and they know my voice. And nothing shall ever take them from me. For my father, which is in Heaven gave them to me because of the shedding of my blood on Calvary. There is something I would like for you to do for me." I answered, "Sure Lord, what would you have me to do?" Jesus answered and said, "There are a lot of other sheep in my fold who are lost and far away from me and cannot hear my voice. I keep calling unto them; but still, they cannot hear. Go and teach my sheep how to listen to my voice. For if they hear you and obey; they will be spared from that awful day of the Lord."

I then said, "I will try to do my best in your service, my Lord if you are with me in spirit and in truth. Then I will know without a doubt that my steps are indeed ordered by the Lord."

I Have Nothing Now to Fear

I am going to rest right here.

I have nothing now to fear.

I know my Lord is always near.

Chorus

So, let the winds blow.

Let the storms come.

Let the floods begin.

I have nothing, no nothing now to fear.

I know, yes I know,

My Lord is always yes always

Going to stay right here.

Even when the trials in life

Come my way,

I will be able to stand up and say

I have nothing now to fear.

Chorus

His peace I have found.

No manner where I abound.

For I know, yes, I know I know I have nothing now to fear.

Repeat the Chorus

We Will Be Together Again

I remember saying I do
And you said you loved me too.
And soon will be together again.

Chorus

For when we meet on that heavenly shore,
We will say our goodbyes no more,
For we will be together again.

Thou today, we must part,
You will always be in my heart.
And soon we will be together again.

Chorus

I remember when we first met

And you said you would never forget

And soon we will be together again.

We will share our memories of old

As we walk together those streets of gold

And then finally will be together again.

<u>There Will Never Be Another You for Me</u>

Today, I looked at a picture of you

On the wall.

It brought back so many memories of you

I can recall,

Memories of you and me

Serving the Lord together and these

Were our precious times.

For you always had the good Lord on

Your mind.

Chorus

<u>There will never be another you for me.</u>

No, there will never be.

You were one of a kind,

For you always had the good Lord

On your mind.

And when you heard His call

You left it all behind.

As I stand by your grave here

I thought we would have more time.

But when you heard the Good Lord's call,

You left it all behind.

And when I hear His call

I too, will leave it all behind.

I then will be joining you

And we shall have then an eternity of time.

I Do Not Want To Wake Up From This Dream of Mine

In this dream, we share all our memories

All our hopes, dreams and fears.

In this dream you are with me

And we share everything.

You did not die

And go to Heaven

And leave me behind.

I do not want to wake up

From this dream of mine.

But I know darling, it is only

A dream.

In this dream, we shared

A kiss or two

And you promised you would

Never leave me behind.

I do not want to wake up

From this dream of mine.

In this dream, we said our vows together

And we said we would love each other forever.

In this dream, you said you loved me

With all your heart

And darling, in this dream of mine,

We never did part.

I know it is only a dream.

So, darling I do not want to wake up

From this dream of mine.

Grannie Is On the Warpath Again

Telling the Devil is never going to win,

Cause she is on the warpath with him.

The Devil is under her feet,

Yes, Grannie is on the warpath again.

Chorus

Grannie is on the warpath again,

Down on the knees, praying,

Amen, Amen.

Yes, Grannie is on the warpath again,

She has got her full armor on

And she is singing the victory song

Cause she has the victory over death and sin.

She is telling the world

Jesus saves and he is coming again.

Yes, Grannie is on the warpath again.

She is praying for all of kin

And praying for salvation for all of her relatives

And friends.

Written: 08/01/2024

<u>Today America is at a crossroads</u>
<u>Between death and life.</u>

Which road will you take?

One will be right

And the other will be a mistake.

One leads to death

And the other leads to life.

One is small and narrow.

The other is large and wide.

One believes in the ways of the Lord.

The other believes in the ways of the

World and all its lies.

What the world claims as love,

God calls sin.

What the world claims as a bunch of cells,

God calls life.

So, choose this day

At the ballot box

The left or the right.

Written: 08/31/2024

Last night I had a dream. I was sitting down in what looked like a huge auditorium or movie theater. There was a man who was in the center Ile, and he was speaking, and I could tell his eyes were on me. He then proceeded to have two people stand from the audience. He begins speaking and he said, "I am looking for a leader to lead us." I just assumed it was just the three of them that he was talking about. He then looked out into the audience, and I could tell again his eyes were on me. I looked around because I could not imagine that it was me that he was referring to. He then stopped by my Ile and asked me to stand up. When I did, He said this to me, "Will you please lead us?" At that moment, I woke up from my dream. I looked at the clock and it was 3:30 am. In the morning.

After I woke up, I ask the Lord what the dream could have meant." He said, "The steps of a righteous man are ordered by the Lord. He went on to say that the man knew that scripture well and he looked into your heart, and he knew that your steps were ordered by the Lord; and because of that, He knew wherever you led them; it would be under the guidance of me. He went on to say, "Child of God, please listen carefully to what I have to say, Yes, I have called you to love all people, but I have also called you as my watchman on the wall, warning my people that there will always be benefits in following my word and there will always be consequences if they do not. I have called you to tell them to read the word for themselves and as your voice is raised up and they read the word, I will draw them unto me and then and only then will they know there is a real Heaven and a real Hell. Go my child and speak now."

Written: 09/07/2024

I was ready for bed because I had been having a lot of pain in my hip that day. I said my nightly prayer and then from within, I heard Jesus speak, "Child, I want to take you to Galilee." I said, "Sure, I would love to go since I was in such pain anyway."

Suddenly we were there. In the spirit, I was feeling no pain, and I was just excited and happy to be there. Jesus saw how happy I looked, and He asked me this question, "Why are you so happy?" I replied, "You know why. Lord, you know everything." He then said, "Yes I do but I want you to tell me yourself."

I said, "I am happy to feel the cool breeze coming off the ocean and I am happy feeling the warm sands between my toes; but most of all I am happy because I am here with you, and this is our favorite place. All I want to do now is walk hand in hand with you, Lord along this beautiful shore."

We walked hand in hand for a little while when Jesus stopped and said, "Child, there is a rock just up ahead where we can sit on and rest before we continue our journey."

As we sit together on the rock, "I said to Jesus, "Jesus, this reminds me of a time in the Bible where you sit on a rock to teach your disciples what we call the "Beatitudes". I then turned and asked Jesus, "Doesn't "beatitude" mean happy, and he replied, "Yes, my child it does."

I then proceeded to repeat one of the beatitudes. I said, "Blessed are the peace makers for they shall see God."

Then, Jesus asked me this question, "Child, do you want to be a peace maker?" I said, "Lord you know I do." He said,

"Then child you are a peace maker when I stir you up to speak for me. Then He asked me this question, "Child, will you do something for me?" I said, "Sure anything as long as I am able." He replied, "Child, you are able. Then He said, "Child, I want you to tell my people that I will visit them in their dreams, and I will draw them unto me, and they will know that day will not come as a thief in the night for them. They will know that I am the Bride Groom coming for my bride, this said the Lord."

Written: 07/13/1995

Dear Mr. President Clinton:

I have written to you before, just before you came into office. I am writing to you again to plead with you to help America return to the ideas of Theodore Roosevelt. He suggested the media, TV and many of the movies were teaching our youth the wrong values. I bet Mr. Roosevelt, if he were alive today, would be so angry at what has happened to our freedom of so-called speech. It has become a freedom to say whatever you feel like. What happened to our freedom to protect our children from the fifth that the media is feeding our youth today? And I do not mean just to flash some warning over the screen or have the parents turn off the TV. It has gotten so bad now that these so-called parents are watching it all themselves, drinking, doping and caring on. Where are the role models for our youth today? There are some but the majority are seen right on the big screen. Heaven help us with all this.

I could not sleep last night, Mr. President because I was awakened by God. I would just like to tell you what I heard from Him. God blesses America when she stands for God, such as when the Constitution of the United States was signed. Our forefathers fought for those freedoms and won because they were praying to God and asking Him for strength and wisdom and most of all, they taught their children the same values. Where are our teachers today, Mr. President? We have homosexuals teaching in some schools and raising our children. If you recall Sodium and Gomorrah in the Bible, it was destroyed because of this sin. God is calling you to come back to Him and make a definite stand for God or else he will remove you as President, do not try to play both sides of the fence. It will never work because you will eventually fall off one of them. Please stand up and use all your influence to bring America back to Godly ways. God never intended this to be, and he is very angry and displeased at America right now for allowing this. How can God bless a people or a nation that teaches its people to use God's name in vain on TV, movie screens, radio, books, or whatever they fell like?

If we want God's true blessings on America, then we need to make some definite stands such as more discipline and punishment procedures such as one strike and you out. Zero tolerance, just as the Job Corps stands for. There should be a law against speaking God's name in vain. The word says, "Thou shalt not take the Lord thy God's name in vain. This means any nation or people that ever freely allow this will someday be punished by God or else God is a liar and the Bible is untrue, which we both know Mr. President is not so. Let's clean up America starting today. We don't know if we shall have it tomorrow, time is running out. Let's start with our mouths and what we teach others to say. Let's start with our eyes and what we teach others to see. For the sake of America. If we the people want God's full blessings, we better start living as God would want us to live, Holy lives before Him. I know this is not Jerusalem, but God's laws are for both the Jews and Gentiles and His prophecies are as well. God's placed on America both a blessing and a curse. If she returns to God, she will be blessed. God will curse America and punish her if she does not return to Him. Mr. President, God has told me that this is your task as President of these United States of America.

Written: 04/21/2004

Dear Mr. President Bush:

I have written to before, but I have not received a response. I am hoping this time will be different. I so much would like to hear from you. You could send me an email message at heavenlygal_99@yahoo.com.

I know you are a very busy man, and I am truly grateful that you are the President of the United States today. It is my opinion that no one should want to elect someone new at this time because our Nation is in such a trial right now. We need to have someone in there who has been close to it all and knows how to handle the difficult situations that may come up. I know our Nation has made a lot of mistakes in the past about security, but I believe with your guidance and help, we can learn a lot. I want to personally thank you for starting Homeland Security. I feel before 911 we as a Nation have become spoiled and have let our guard down; never thinking it could ever happen here. That now, however, has changed. And since 9/11 we the American people are more cautious about things. One thing that does really bother me is this blame game the Commission and the media is playing. Don't they realize that they are just giving fire to the enemy by further dividing us as a Nation? Abraham Lincoln once said, "A house divided against itself will not stand." We must stand together and defeat our enemies. I believe we are fighting against evil powers because God's word proclaims, "We wrestle not against flesh and blood, but against principalities, against powers, against the rulers of the darkness of this world, against spiritual wickedness in high places. Wherefore, God has said that we must take on the whole armor of God that we may be able to withstand in the evil day, and having done all, to stand up His word.

Respectfully,

Emma L. Cross

Written: 11/05/2004

Dear Mr. President Bush:

I want to thank you for the letter you sent me on June 15, 2004. A Lot has happened since then. The reason I am writing to you again is two-fold. First, I want to congratulate you on your victory of returning to the White House for your second term. I see you are following in the footsteps of your father. However, I know you are indeed your own man. You have certainly proved that in the way you have handled the leadership as our Commander and Chief of this great land.

The second reason is because I need to tell you about a divine revelation that I received on November 1, 2004; the day before the election. I was sitting at my desk at work and I pondered this question: "Who would win this election tomorrow?" In my heart I knew who I wanted to win, but I wanted to hear from the Lord. The spirit of the Lord came to me in a still small voice and said, "You know President Clinton because you wrote to him, you know President Bush because you wrote to him, but you do not know Kerry." I replied from within, "That is true." Then the spirit of the Lord said, "It shall be Bush, him I know, Kerry I do not." I am sure the Lord did not mean any disrespect to Mr. Kerry. I feel in my heart the Lord was answering me in a way I would be able to understand naturally.

Following those words, the spirit of the Lord reminded me of the same scripture He gave me at 3:00 a.m. in the morning right after your address to the Nation. The scripture found in 2nd Chronicles 7:14. Afterwards, I heard the voice of the Lord say, "Child, my people which are called by my name have humbled themselves and prayed and have sought me out and

I heard their cries. I will forgive their sin. and will heal their land. Then the spirit of the Lord said, "My Church, my people will awake from slumber arise and dress for the Glorious occasion" Mr. President I did not realize all of this until after the election was over. Then I heard how people of all faiths came together to do their God-given duty and voted. Then the rest became History.

Respectfully,

Emma L. Cross

Written: 03/10/2024

Dear Mr. President Biden:

Mr. President, I mean you no harm. I am a 74-year-old widow woman that has trusted in the Lord for over 50 years, and I know when He speaks to me and when He does, I try to obey. I did not want to write this, but the spirit of the Lord kept urging me too. Just know that nothing, no nothing will ever be done by my hand. I am just His messenger.

I was in the spirit on the Lord's Day, and I heard Him say to me, "Go my child, and warn him with these words.

I am the Alpha and the Omega, the beginning and the end. I am the Lord; your God and I change not. I am the same today, yesterday and forever. I am not pleased with your ways. In one day out of revenge, and by the stroke of your hand you brought judgement down upon my people. If you do not repent; it will be by my hand, Almighty God and in one day will I bring down that same judgment to you. You have transgressed my laws. You once were a man of faith but now you are a worldly person. You made a mockery out of my sanctity of marriage. No one mocks me. Whatever you sow; so shall you reap. I said," for this cause, man should leave his mother and father and cling to his wife, and they should become one flesh and multiply after their kind. In the garden, I said, "it is not good for man to be alone, and I placed Adam in a deep sleep and then took one his ribs and made woman. You believe in the way of the world, and you are a stumbling block to me because you teach others to go against my laws. Another way you have transgressed my laws is condoning the very actions that caused me to destroy two cities. You now teach others to do the same. And lastly, you carry innocent blood on your hands for you stole my right to life and gave it over to woman which is my creation. Therefore, if you do not repent, I will come quickly. You are old now and death will come soon, but after death will come judgment. I will judge the things you have done in my Name. As you can see now, where you will be for eternity. If a man gains the entire world and loses his soul or what shall a man give in exchange for his soul? Thus, saith the Lord."

These are the words of the Lord to you this day and I pray that you will heed them. I have in the past written similar letters to other presidents and others as the Lord enabled me to do so. I wrote President Clinton and told him that the Lord said if he returned this nation back to God; he would be blessed; but if he did not; he would be cursed and be removed. He did not listen, and he was almost removed. I wrote President Bush, and he did not listen and 9-11 occurred and also the Challenger. I wrote the Supreme Court because the Lord told me there was a world wind coming and that He judged them and found them wanting, He said they judged by man's law and not by His when they chose to put into law the same sex marriage act. Shortly after that one of them was found dead in a hotel room.

I have written this for one reason and that is God's word said, "Behold to obey is better than sacrifice." I want to know that when I leave this world no manner how hard the task, He asked me to do that I will have done the best to obey Him. I want to hear Him say these words to me, "Well done, my good and faithful servant, enter now into the joys of your Lord." I know without a doubt that my late husband heard them, and he left this world behind to go and be with Him forever and ever with the Lord. He never compromised with the world. He stood firm in his faith to the very end. That is what I want for you. You may have started out late, but it is never too late with our Lord. He is always ready to forgive.

Mr. President, I pray that you too will want to hear those same words when your time on this earth is done. May God Bless you and may God continue to bless this great Nation of ours.

Respectfully Yours,

Emma L. Cross

Written: 07/20, 2024

Dear Mr. President Trump,

I am writing to you this day to ask you and Vice President Vance to let go of the past regarding the stolen election. The reason being, God did not want you to be the President then. He wants you to be the President in this term. I have written to you many times before. I am the 75-year-old widow woman that many would say is the modern-day Joan of Arc. She had a passion for France and heard from God. I have a passion for America, and I also hear from God. I am not crazy or senile and I can bring you proof of what I say. You can even back it up with other modern- day men of God such as the late Clement or Johnathan Cahn.

Ever since I was a small girl, I have heard it said that if God does not punish America, He would have to apologize to Sidon and Gomorrah. All the time growing up, I never saw any reason that would occur until several years ago.

One night many years ago, we had a special prayer for an upcoming election for our president; while I was praying a vision of Abraham and Lott of the Bible came to my mind. I did not understand until under the anointing of the Holy Spirit I was told to write to President Clinton and told him that God had placed on America both a blessing and a cursing; If he returns America back to God, he would be blessed but if he did not, he would be cursed and be removed. He almost was removed. Next, I warned President Bush because during the war, I was wakening up at 3:00 a.m. and under the anointing of the Holy Spirit again, I wrote asking the Lord if there was anything I could do to help America then. I said that I could not sew a flag like Betsy Ross did. At that moment, I heard the Lord say, "Child get down upon your knees and pray for America. I did and I heard Him say, "Child it will be easier for a gay to come out and say I am Gay then it would be for a person to say I am a Christian and I heard from God today. They would think you were crazy and want to put you away."

I wrote to President Bush, but he did not heed the warning either. I kept praying, one night at 2:00 a.m. I was awakened by God and He said," Ye shall have a black president, but the Church will be going." I did not understand then and after that I started watching the signs as the birth pains began. I watched as President Obama put into place the no ask, no tell in the military. I begged him to speak with the late Billy Graham, but he did not. When it came time for a new election, I told the Lord I did not want to know who the next president would be. The voice of the Lord then said, "The handwriting is already on the wall." I knew then that President Obama would be president for the second term. In his second term, evil really began. On the very day, he got the Supreme Court to pass the same sex marriage act and shamelessly portrayed the Whitehouse in Rainbow colors. The rainbow in the Bible stood for God's covenant to mankind and it was like a slap in the face of God. I knew it would make God angry. On that very day at work, the Holy Spirit gave me a poem titled, "Judgment Is Coming to America."

One night I woke up again and was told by God that there was a whirlwind coming and I wrote to the Supreme Court and told them all I have said before with the warning. They did not listen. I kept praying for America. Then another day came for another election. At first, I believed it would be Ted

Cruz because his face came before me in the middle of the and the Lord said that this is a man of great valor. I had never seen him before that day and the next day I was on the computer and I saw his face for the first time and he was coming to defend the bathroom issue here in Houston, Texas. That issue alone was warned by God to me. One day, I was at Walmart returning some items and suddenly, I heard the Lord tell mem "Child turn towards the bathrooms." I obeyed and then he said, "Child a man will go into the restroom with your little girl." At that point I thought I was hearing thins not correctly because my daughter was grown and had children of her that was also grown. That Sunday morning, I asked my pastor about it and he said that who know, it could happen and within 3 months later, it almost did if Ted Cruz had not come to our aide. I kept praying and then I saw you on the internet and God told me that you would be our next president. I looked up on the internet about other prophecies about you and it confirmed that you would be the President. It also said you would have a second term which I believed was going to happen then, but it did not. I was heartbroken when you did not win but the Lord gave me a poem titled, "The People Are Praying." Then when you took office you did something that no other president did. You moved the US Embassy to Jerusalem. This was what God wanting you to do for his people and the world at that time. After praying about why you did not win the election, I realized it was not the right time, but this time is. I believe during your second term you will bring peace to America and peace to Isreal and Palestine. I also believe that during your term Israel will build or begin to build the third temple. This is the most exciting time to live for God is about to do something that only God can do.

I told you about the letter the Lord had me to write warning President Biden, and what would happen to him in one day and as you know it is happening even now.

So, I have said all of this to tell you to forget the past election. I loved your speech on unity, and I heard nothing but love from your soul. I told you once that God is in control. And He is using you for His Glory. So just set back and relax and enjoy the ride. Your pilot is more than able to see that you land on your feet every time. It is time to give God all the Glory for soon and very soon the book of Revelations will be fulfilled. May God Bless and keep you and Vice President Vance and may God bless this great Nation under God in a land of the free and the home of the brave.

Respectfully Yours,

Emma L. Cross

We Learned To Give First As God Gave and Received Something Where There Was Once Nothing

I would like to share with you this article that I was featured in that came from "The Oral Roberts Abundant Life Magazine" of December 1976.

It was a couple of weeks before Christmas when 1 was visiting my mother, and before I left, she gave me a copy of the ABUNDANT LIFE magazine. I didn't think much of it and when I got home, I put it on top of the television, never intending to read it. That night my husband was listening to some records in the living room and-as I walked back to my room, I automatically picked up the magazine and began to read the testimony about a couple who had given a gift as a seed and had received a miracle from God. I paused after reading the testimony and seemed to feel the Lord urging me to start giving as they did. At the time, all my husband and I had was our Christmas. I reconsidered the idea. Perhaps it was just me; the testimony had deeply touched me and naturally I thought it was God speaking. I thought, I shouldn't be selfish, but then why should we give our Christmas away when we have so little this year ourselves? After all, my husband was out of work and things were hard enough as it was. I tried to put the thought out of my mind but couldn't. One week later I sat down to watch the Oral Roberts television program when the urging came back to me. Finally, I said, "Lord, if this is you telling me to start giving the Seed-Faith way, then let this man say something about giving that I will know You are speaking to me." The Lord wasn't long in answering. His very first words were, "When you feel you are at point-zero you can give a prayer, or friendship, or compassion, or time or money- everyone has something to give - and whatever you give God will multiply back to you." I knew without a doubt that God wanted us to start giving the Seed-Faith way as quickly as God answered my first request,

He fulfilled His promise to return more than what we gave. The very next day at work we were told that the following month we would receive a $50 raise. Then, the following Saturday I stayed with my cousin's mother and daughter while she worked. My aunt was sick and unable to take care of herself, so I helped her. As I washed and combed her tousled hair, God opened my eyes to the fact, that there is so much to be done and so little time to do it. I didn't realize the impact of this revelation until the next morning when I got word that my aunt had had a heart attack during the night. Immediately I prayed to God for a second chance to do His work. And again He answered my prayer -- that very night my aunt was brought home. With all that has happened to me and my family in this short time, I can hardly wait to seed for my next miracle. I know I've discovered the beginning of God's mighty power in my daily life. Thank you for feeding my soul through your letters, your magazine, and your telecasts, Brother Roberts, and encouraging my heart and praying for me and my family.

DECEMBER 1976

Mrs. Emma Lee Cross

ETERNAL HOME

As you can see by reading my story, ever since I accepted Jesus into my heart, I have longed to go home one day to my eternal home, where I will be forever with Jesus Christ, my Lord. The scripture states in 1st Corinthians 2:9, "Eye has not seen, nor ear has not heard, nor have entered into the heart of man the things which God has prepared for those who love Him." Revelations 21: 21, "And the twelve gates were twelve pearls: every several gates were of one pearl: and the street of the city was pure gold, as if were transparent glass."

The scripture also states in Revelation 21:4, "And God shall wipe away all tears from their eyes: and there shall be no more death, neither sorrow nor pain: for the former things are passed away." No more saying goodbyes to our loved ones ever again. And all those who accepted Jesus Christ into their hearts will all be together on that glorious day. One day soon that trumpet is going to sound just like the Bible said it would, and then, brother and sister, we will be homeward bound. Here are the words of an old gospel song that I am feeling right now. "I Have Never Been This Homesick Before."

There is a light in the window.

The table's spread in splendor.

Someone's standing by the open door.

I can see a crystal river.

I must be near forever.

See, I've never been this homesick before.

I see the bright light shine.

It is just about home time.

I can see my father standing at the door.

This world has been a wilderness.

I'm ready for deliverance.

Lord, I've never been this homesick before.

I can see the family gather

Sweet faces, all familiar

And no one's old or feeble anymore.

And my lonesome heart is cryin' Think I'll spread my wings for flyin'

I've never been this homesick before.

Another song I would like to share with you today is titled: "Thank You for Giving to the Lord" by Ray Boltz.

This was one of my husband's favorite songs to play during our services at the nursing homes in Houston, Texas. And now since his death, it has also become one of mine. Here are the words of the song:

I dreamed I went to heaven, and you were there with me.

We walked upon the streets of gold beside the crystal sea.

We heard the angels singing and someone called your name:

We turned and saw this young man and he was smiling as he came.

And he said, "Friend, you may not know me now" then he said,

"But wait, you use to teach me Sunday school when I was only eight and one day you said that prayer, I ask Jesus in my heart."

Thank you for giving to the Lord.

I am a life that was changed.

Thank you for giving to the Lord.

I am so glad you gave.

Then another man stood before you, he said, "Remember the time.

A missionary came to your church, his picture made you cry:

You didn't' have much money, but you gave it anyway.

Jesus took that gift you gave and that is why I'm here today."

One by one, they came as far as the eye could see.

Each life somehow touched by your generosity.

Little things that you had done, sacrifices made,

Unnoticed on the earth, in heaven now proclaimed.

I know that up in heaven, you are not supposed to cry

But I am almost sure there were tears in your eyes.

As Jesus took you hand, you stood before the Lord.

He said, "My child look around you; great is your reward."

That song means more to me today than ever. This is my deepest prayer that someday, when I am in Heaven, someone will come to me saying, "I read your book, and I accepted Jesus Christ into my heart. I am here today because you shared your story. Thank you for giving to the Lord. Reader, you may think this is the end, but it is only the beginning when you are living a more abundantly life in Jesus Christ.

www.ingramcontent.com/pod-product-compliance
Lightning Source LLC
Chambersburg PA
CBHW071124130526
44590CB00056B/1745